The Time-Life Gardener's Guide

FLOWERING HOUSEPLANTS

A

BOOK

The Time-Life Gardener's Guide

FLOWERING HOUSEPLANTS

TIME-LIFE BOOKS, ALEXANDRIA, VIRGINIA

CONTENTS

1

THE INDOOR ENVIRONMENT

2

CARE AND CULTIVATION

3

NEW PLANTS FROM OLD

Among houseplants, flowering plants are the stellar performers. While foliage plants provide a background of green throughout the year, flowering plants command attention with showy, if brief, bursts of color. And because blossoming is a demanding activity, flowering plants generally require more nurturing than do their perennially green counterparts.

This volume is intended as a guide for growing flowering houseplants. Chapters on care and maintenance cover the particular needs of blossoming plants confined to the house. A chapter on propagation details a variety of ways in which to reproduce flowering plants, allowing you some control over the results. To prepare plants for exhibition, special sections on training, cleaning and transporting plants are included, and a chapter on troubleshooting will help you to deal with plants' seasonal changes, as well as any threats to their well-being from insects and diseases. The Dictionary of Flowering Houseplants at the end of the book provides detailed descriptions of more than 100 genera and furnishes information on their individual needs; it will help you both to choose plants carefully and to give the best possible care to the ones you already have.

HOUSEPLANTS ON DISPLAY

WORKING IN TANDEM WITH NATURE

DICTIONARY OF HOUSEPLANTS

1
THE INDOOR ENVIRONMENT

Most flowering houseplants are native to the tropics and the subtropics, where factors such as temperature, humidity, the length of the days and the intensity of the sun's light remain largely constant. Such plants are extremely sensitive to changes in their environment. While the temperature in most homes may be kept relatively stable from season to season by heating and air conditioning, other environmental factors—such as humidity and the duration and intensity of light—can change markedly from one season to the next, affecting plants' propensity to blossom and their overall health.

   This chapter describes the conditions that flowering houseplants need in order to flourish: growing medium, water, humidity and light. In addition, it suggests ways in which you can control your indoor climate to promote the beauty and well-being of your plants. The chapter begins by showing how to make potting mixes to meet the needs of plants as different as cactus and African violets. A subsequent section on watering shows how to use a capillary mat to water plants from below—perhaps the surest way to avoid both under- and over-watering. For homes where dryness is a seasonal, or a chronic, problem, there are suggestions on how to increase the moisture in indoor air. Finally, a section on light—which is especially crucial to the health of blossoming plants—shows where plants should be placed in relation to windows with various exposures in order to receive the light they need. For homes that do not receive sufficient sunlight, there are directions for using an artificial light source to meet the needs of even the most light-thirsty plants.

IDEAL GROWING MEDIA FOR INDOOR PLANTS

Most flowering houseplants need a potting mixture that performs several functions at the same time. It should be light, so it will let in lots of oxygen, hold plenty of moisture and yet drain well. It should also have a slightly acid chemistry.

Such a mixture is easy to concoct at home with ingredients readily found at garden supply centers. Garden shops also sell ready-made commercial mixes, but not all are first-rate—you have a better chance of maintaining good quality if you make your own, as shown opposite. You can store any left over for future use.

The mix consists of equal amounts of three main ingredients. First is sphagnum peat moss, which retains water and nutrients. Next is vermiculite, a crumbly substance made from mica, which also helps hold moisture and improves aeration. Third is perlite—ground-up volcanic ore that drains swiftly and improves aeration as well. The one other ingredient is dolomite lime. Adding 1 tablespoon to each gallon of mix counteracts the moss's acidity, bringing the mix's overall acid level down to about 6.5 on the pH scale—just on the acid side of pH 7, which is neutral.

The mix contains no garden soil whatever —for good reason. Garden soil may contain weeds (or their seeds), bacteria, fungi, nematodes and insects. The lack of soil has a drawback: namely, the nutrients that real soil provides are absent. But this is easily remedied by regular applications of all-purpose houseplant fertilizer, as explained on pages 24-25.

Two types of houseplants need growing mixes that differ slightly from this standard one. Cactus plants and other succulents do best in a porous, well-drained medium; African violets and similar plants prefer a richer and more acidic medium. Formulas for both are given in the box at bottom right.

Growing exuberantly in a soilless mixture especially enriched with extra fertilizer, a primrose produces a characteristic rounded cluster of bright red-and-yellow blooms. The basic indoor planting mix can be adjusted to the needs of particular species.

1 To make a generous supply of potting mix, pour equal amounts of perlite, peat moss and vermiculite into a good-sized bucket or a tub that has been washed with a mild solution of water and household bleach. Be sure all the ingredients are sterile—it should say so on the bags—so that you do not introduce disease-carrying organisms into your mixture. Then add lime, 1 tablespoon per gallon of mixture, to raise the pH level. Mix thoroughly.

2 Keep any extra planting mixture from contamination in a sealed container. Either place the lid on the container if it has one, or pour the leftover mix into a sturdy plastic bag and close it with a twist tie. Label the mix and indicate the date. The medium should be usable for several months. ☐

TWO ALTERNATIVE MIXES

The planting mixture needed by most cactus plants and other succulents is a sandier, faster-draining version of the basic mix described above and at left. Simply substitute 1 part builder's sand for the usual vermiculite. Everything else—the perlite, sphagnum peat moss and lime—remains the same. The medium for African violets, begonias and other houseplants with delicate roots is also a variation on the regular mixture. Use 2 parts sphagnum peat moss instead of one, adding them to the usual 1 part perlite and 1 part vermiculite. This makes the mixture more acid and helps it retain needed water.

WAYS TO WATER: FROM ABOVE AND FROM BELOW

Plants need water to produce carbohydrates through photosynthesis, to transport nutrients to existing tissues and to keep stems and leaves sturdy. They absorb it primarily through their roots. How much they need is determined by several factors: the type of plant (fleshy-leaved plants need less water than thin-leaved ones); the time of year (plants generally need more water when they are growing than when they are dormant); the size and material of the pot (plants in large pots need less frequent watering than plants in small pots, and plastic pots retain moisture better than clay); and the type of growing medium (peat moss and vermiculite hold moisture better than perlite or sand).

Most home gardeners water their plants by pouring water on top of the growing medium; this is known as surface irrigation. If you use this method, make sure the root zone is thoroughly moistened; keep pouring until water seeps from the drainage hole. Allow the pot to drain for 10 minutes, then set it on a saucer. Never let plants sit in water for long periods; this can cause root rot.

An alternative method, known as bottom watering *(below and opposite),* allows roots to take up the water they need via capillary action. Garden stores sell capillary mats (made of an absorbent cottonlike material) that sit beneath plants in watertight trays. If you use this method, you will need to prevent light from shining on the mat *(Step 2),* or algae will develop. Give each plant a good surface watering under a faucet once a month to remove accumulated mineral salts. Hold the pot under the tap until water comes from the drainage hole; let drain for 10 minutes, then repeat. A variation on this system will keep your plants watered when you are away *(box, opposite).*

This pink blooming cyclamen draws the water it needs from a moistened capillary mat that covers the bottom of an ornamental ceramic saucer.

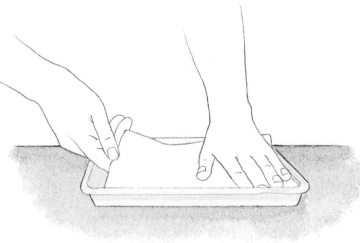

1 To set up a bottom-watering system, you will need a watertight tray and a capillary mat. You can buy a mat at a garden store or make your own from a piece of felt. Cut the mat to size, moisten it and lay it on the bottom of the tray.

2 To prevent unsightly algae from growing on the moist fibers on the surface of the mat, cut a sheet of black plastic the same size as the mat, cut a hole in the plastic to fit the bottom of each pot and lay the plastic sheet on top of the capillary mat *(right)*. Without light, algae cannot grow.

3 Set the plants in the lined tray so that each pot is centered in one of the holes in the plastic sheet *(above)*. The roots will absorb water from the mat through the drainage holes in the pots. Keep the mat moist at all times; check daily and add water as needed.

4 To moisten the mat, lift up one plant and pour water through the hole in the plastic sheet *(above)*. Add just enough water to moisten the entire mat evenly. Every month or so, remove all the plants from the tray and give them a thorough surface watering under a tap to leach out any mineral salts that may have accumulated. □

WATERING PLANTS WHEN YOU'RE AWAY

By using a bottom-watering system with a capillary mat, you can ensure that your plants get the water they need when you are away from home for up to one week. The setup differs somewhat from the daily watering system described above. Cut a piece of capillary mat large enough to accommodate all your plants on a flat surface, and submerge one end of the mat in an adjacent water basin; the mat will absorb moisture evenly so long as water remains in the basin. Fill the basin with water and set the plants on the mat. If the flat surface needs protection from moisture, cut a piece of plastic to size and place it beneath the mat.

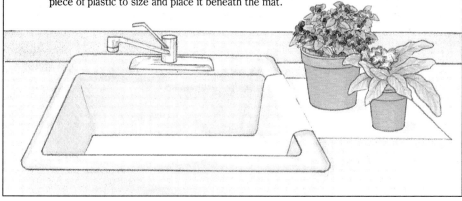

TRANSPIRATION: BALANCING THE WATER BUDGET

Flowering primulas, ferns and a Christmas cactus make use of the humidity provided by water in the pebble-filled tray beneath the pot. As the water constantly evaporates from the tray and enters the surrounding air, it slows the rate at which the plants lose moisture to the air in the process known as transpiration.

Proper watering of houseplants involves more than just keeping the growing medium moist. You also have to pay attention to the air around the plant—because in opening its pores to take in carbon dioxide from the air, the plant loses moisture. This process of exchanging carbon dioxide and water is called transpiration.

In an effort to replace the moisture lost in transpiration, a plant's roots absorb water from the growing medium. But if the air is very dry, the leaves may lose water faster than the roots can replace it, and the plant will eventually wilt. The solution is to slow down the rate of transpiration.

To accomplish this, it helps to understand the relationship between the moisture content of the air and air temperature. The warmer the air, the more moisture it can hold as water vapor. Relative humidity measures the moisture content of the air compared with the maximum amount of moisture the air *could* hold at a given temperature. When air cannot hold any more water vapor, it is said to be saturated; saturated air has a relative humidity of 100 percent.

Air that is not saturated will cause water to evaporate from all available surfaces, including a plant's leaves. To slow down transpiration, you must raise the relative humidity. Relative humidity is measured with an instrument called a hygrometer. Most houseplants do best at a relative humidity of about 60 percent; succulents prefer a relative humidity between 30 percent and 40 percent; tropical plants like a relative humidity of about 80 percent.

One way to increase humidity is to group several plants together to create a more humid microclimate; each plant benefits from the moisture evaporating from the others. Or you can keep plants on a tray having an inch or two of pebbles on the bottom and add water to just below the tops of the pebbles. As the water evaporates, the humidity level around the plants increases. Check daily and replenish the water as needed.

WATER IN, WATER OUT

When water from a watering can is poured onto the growing medium of a potted plant, it seeps down to the root zone. There it is absorbed by the roots, drawn up the stem and distributed to tissues throughout the plant. When the plant opens its pores to take in carbon dioxide from the air, the plant loses moisture. The entire process is known as transpiration. When the air around a plant gets too dry, the plant's rate of transpiration increases. □

PUTTING PLANTS
IN THE RIGHT LIGHT

The buttery yellow blossoms and rich green foliage of this hibiscus drink in the direct sunlight needed to produce and maintain a strong, healthy plant.

Indoor light is measured in levels of intensity, and falls into three categories: direct sunlight, bright indirect sunlight and limited sunlight. *Direct sunlight* is what shines unobstructed through a window that faces south, east or west. Plants placed in such a window are bathed in sunlight all or most of the day. *Bright indirect sunlight* is found wherever the intensity of sunlight is diminished by curtains, by outside obstructions like trees or buildings, or by distance; the farther away from the window, the less intense the light, even if the window is unobstructed. *Limited sunlight* is found near an unobstructed north-facing window, and near south-, east- and west-facing windows that receive no direct or bright indirect sun. It is insufficient for flowering houseplants to thrive.

If you cannot place your flowering houseplants in a sufficiently sunny window, you can install two 40-watt fluorescent bulbs—one a "cool" white bulb that supplies the blue and violet wavelengths necessary for foliage development, the other a "warm" white bulb that supplies the red and orange necessary for flowers to develop. The bulbs should be placed 6 inches above mature plants, and about 2 inches above seedlings. A timer can be programmed to turn the lights on and off as required.

HOW THE LIGHT FALLS

The diagram below illustrates the distances at which direct, bright indirect and limited sunlight reach houseplants, depending upon where they are situated in relation to windows facing north, south, east or west. Most flowering houseplants blossom poorly where there is only limited sunlight. But direct sunlight can be too intense, and during the summer months you may have to filter sunlight in south-facing windows to protect houseplants from being scorched. Check the Dictionary of Houseplants *(pages 72-137)* for the specific light requirements of individual species. □

———————————— DIRECT SUNLIGHT

— — — — — — BRIGHT INDIRECT SUNLIGHT

· · · · · · · · · · LIMITED SUNLIGHT

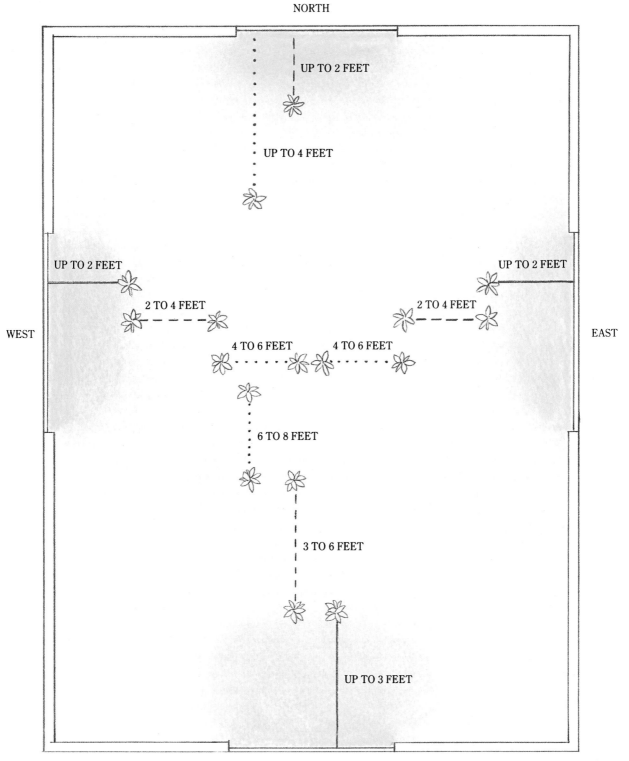

NORTH

UP TO 2 FEET

UP TO 4 FEET

WEST

UP TO 2 FEET

UP TO 2 FEET

2 TO 4 FEET

2 TO 4 FEET

4 TO 6 FEET

4 TO 6 FEET

EAST

6 TO 8 FEET

3 TO 6 FEET

UP TO 3 FEET

SOUTH

2
CARE
AND CULTIVATION

Given a sunny spot and an occasional watering, many flowering houseplants will remain healthy. But getting them to produce abundant, colorful blossoms may require some additional encouragement. Conditions that inspire root and foliage development often work against blossom production, since a plant has only a limited amount of energy to expend upon growth. The trick, of course, is being able to maintain a balance; the information in this chapter is intended to help you to balance your plants' needs where both health and appearance are concerned.

Since flowering houseplants spend their lives in containers, the size, type and appearance of those containers are important considerations. A section on potting tells when and how to repot plants that have outgrown their pots, as well as how to display them to best advantage by placing them in decorative pots or by grouping several together in a single container. Some plants, such as orchids, require special attention when it comes to potting; their needs are covered in a separate section.

Because their roots are confined to a small space, potted plants can receive only limited amounts of the nutrients they need to survive from the soil or medium in which they grow. Periodic applications of fertilizer are necessary for healthy plants, and this chapter will guide you as to the best type and the right amount of fertilizer for specific plants' needs. Advice on cleaning, pruning and deadheading your plants will help you to keep them looking fit, and may actually increase their blooming. When insects attack, a section on controlling them without insecticides will prove useful.

Some plants require special treatment in order to bloom. Some need a period of cold to bring them to life; others simply need warmth and exposure to strong sunlight. A section on forcing potted bulbs provides the details for urging spring blossomers such as tulips, crocuses and hyacinths to bloom indoors in wintertime.

REPOTTING PLANTS TO MAKE ROOM FOR THE ROOTS

Maintaining healthy and shapely houseplants calls for some occasional repotting. Vigorous plants sooner or later become too large for their containers, and they will not stay vigorous unless given room to continue growing. But, moving plants into bigger pots brings several benefits besides giving the roots more space: fresh growing medium, more oxygen, better drainage—in short, something like a fresh start in life.

It is not hard to tell when a plant needs to be moved to a larger pot. The distress signals are top-heavy growth that looks too large for the pot and roots growing through the drainage hole in the pot's bottom. Whatever signal alerts you, remove the plant from its container and look at the root ball. If it looks compacted and cramped, reach for a new pot.

The fresh pot should be about 2 inches larger in diameter at the rim than the old one; this will allow enough space for the roots to grow, but not so much space that the plant will spend its energy growing roots and have none left for producing blossoms. The only real trick to repotting, described below and opposite, is positioning the root ball properly in the new container. Its top should be about ¾ inch below the container rim. If it sits higher than that, water will spill over the edge of the pot; if lower, the roots will not have the full benefit of the additional room.

A houseplant will often look handsomer if it is "double-potted"—that is, if the terra-cotta or plastic pot that holds the growing medium is placed inside a more elegant, decorative container. The container you choose may have no drainage holes or it may be a bit too roomy. How to deal with these minor difficulties is explained in the box at the bottom of the facing page.

A velvety red gloxinia luxuriates in a good-sized terra-cotta pot. Gloxinias benefit from occasional repotting; it gives their tubers room to grow.

1 To repot a plant that has outgrown its container, start by choosing a pot with a diameter 2 inches larger, and putting a small amount of sterile growing medium into the pot.

2 Remove the plant from its pot. If the root ball sticks—compacted ones often do—turn the pot upside down and knock it against a hard surface *(right)*. Then, supporting the stems between your fingers, tug on the pot and twist it until it comes free. Cradle the freed plant carefully. If the root ball is tightly wound, work your fingers into the soil and between the roots to loosen them up.

3 Center the plant in the new pot so that the root ball's top is ¾ inch below the pot's rim. Adjust the depth if necessary by adding more growing medium to the bottom of the pot or by removing the excess. Fill in around the root ball with handfuls of new, fresh growing medium. Water generously to give the transplanted roots a good moist start. □

A POT WITHIN A POT

Choice houseplants that deserve showing off can be double-potted: that is, a plant growing in a plain clay or plastic growing pot can be placed inside a showier container such as the brass one at right. The main drawback of decorative containers is that they usually lack drainage holes, and water that pools in the bottom of such pots can damage them. This can be remedied simply by placing a piece of plastic or a saucer in the bottom of the container to protect it. If you need to raise the height of the inside pot, place a couple of small wooden blocks underneath the saucer. If you want to disguise the inner pot, fill in between the rims of the two pots with sphagnum moss.

DIFFERENT ORCHIDS, DIFFERENT WAYS TO REPOT

Orchids bought at greenhouses and by mail often grow well in their original pots for several months. But like most other houseplants, they eventually outgrow their containers and need to be repotted. With such exotic plants, this takes extra care and knowledge.

First, there are several types of orchids and they need somewhat different treatment. About half the species are terrestrials that, as the name implies, grow in the earth. These plants can be repotted in any regular houseplant potting mixture that drains well *(pages 18-19)*.

Most orchids grown as houseplants, however, are the odder epiphytes—plants that in the wild grow aboveground by means of aerial roots that attach themselves to trees. There are two types of epiphytes—monopodial ("single-footed"), which have one main stem rising from a cluster of roots, and sympodial, which have multiple stems emerging from a horizontal rhizome. These stems, called pseudobulbs, store water and nutrients.

Epiphytic orchids should be repotted in a very light, fast-draining medium so their roots get plenty of oxygen. Shredded fir bark works well; so do commercial orchid-growing media.

Orchids should be repotted when their leaves and roots spill well beyond the edges of the old container, or when the potting medium shrinks or begins to deteriorate—but never when the plant is in bloom.

The illustrations below and opposite show the best method of dividing and repotting a sympodial cattleya orchid. The box at far right describes how to repot a monopodial moth orchid.

Flourishing in direct light, a cattleya hybrid produces its characteristic sprays of brilliantly colored petals. These orchids grow a top-heavy 12 to 18 inches tall with heavy, leathery leaves and need to be held in place by metal clips that loop over the rhizome and the edge of the pot.

1 To begin repotting a sympodial or multistemmed orchid, gently pry the plant from its pot, running a knife blade around the inside of the pot if necessary. Then, using your fingers, remove as much as possible of the old growing medium from the roots.

2 Reduce the size of the root system by snipping off dead roots and trimming back long ones with sterilized pruning shears. Cut and remove any dry, dead or discolored large stems—the pseudobulbs, which are at the rear of the horizontal rhizome. Be sure to leave at least three leaves and pseudobulbs and the new shoot that forms between flowerings at the rhizome's tip.

3 Position the new plant at the inside edge of a clean pot so the rhizome is ½ inch below the rim of the pot. The plant should be off-center so the oldest pseudobulb touches one side of the pot and the new shoot has room to grow before reaching the opposite side. Holding the plant in this position, fill in around the roots with fir bark or some other suitable medium.

4 When the pot is filled with fir bark, make sure the orchid will stand up by using an orchid clip; because the planting medium is so light, top-heavy sympodial orchids tend to flop over. Insert the clip over the rim of the pot, as shown, and press it down over the rhizome. Water generously, but be sure the pot is draining well since orchids do badly in a sodden growing medium. □

REFRESHING A MONOPODIAL ORCHID

With no rhizomes or pseudobulbs to be carefully positioned and clipped in place, monopodial orchids are easier to repot than sympodial orchids. After shaking the old potting mixture from the roots, simply center the plant in a new container that is 2 inches larger than the previous one. The base of the stem and the lowest leaves should be about ½ inch below the container rim. Fill in around the roots with shredded fir bark or a commercial orchid-growing medium.

AN INDOOR GARDEN IN A BASKET

Few gardening projects bring such immediate gratification as a miniature indoor garden. You combine a well-matched assortment of houseplants in an attractive container large enough to hold them all comfortably—and stand back to admire your handiwork.

By their very nature, arrangements of this sort are temporary; plants that die or grow out of scale must be replaced by new plants. Nevertheless, a little forethought can help you get the most out of a minigarden.

Start with plants that look as if they belong together naturally. They should be young and compact, and have similar preferences for light, water and growing medium. This does *not* mean forsaking variety. There are many compatible foliage plants that offer subtle but pleasing contrasts in color, scale and texture. For color, add one or two of the smaller flowering houseplants—such as African violets, begonias and primroses.

Flowering plants need strong light to continue blooming, and will rarely thrive under conditions that suit foliage plants. In anticipation of this problem, leave flowering plants in their individual pots when you insert them in the garden. That way, as soon as a plant stops flowering you can easily lift it out and replace it with another in full bloom.

You can create a miniature garden in virtually any kind of container that catches your fancy—a woven basket, a plastic tub, a ceramic bowl. If the container is not waterproof, line it with a sheet of plastic before adding soil or growing medium. Gardens in shallow containers without drainage holes should be watered sparingly to reduce the risk of root rot.

White cyclamen, vining ivy and peace lily plants share a woven grapevine basket. The plants provide a contrast in styles, but they have similar preferences for light, water and growing medium, so they are excellent companions in such an arrangement.

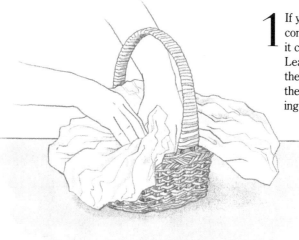

1 If you are using a non-waterproof container, like a woven basket, line it completely with a piece of plastic. Leave the excess plastic draped over the sides. Cover the bottom of the container with a layer of growing medium.

2 Remove the foliage plants you are using from their pots and set each plant in the container *(left)*. Arrange them in a pleasing design, taking into account size, color and texture. Fill in around the plants with more growing medium. Make sure all plants sit about ½ inch below the rim of the container; adjust the depth of the growing medium if necessary.

3 Insert each flowering houseplant, pot and all, in the container where it will contribute most to the overall design *(right)*. Stand back to view the arrangement; if any of the foliage plants obstruct the flowering plant, cut back the foliage to remove the obstruction.

4 Trim away the excess plastic around the outside of the container. Fill in any gaps around the inside of the container with sphagnum moss. Water sparingly. Do not water again until the foliage begins to wilt. □

REGULAR FERTILIZING FOR VIGOROUS HOUSEPLANTS

Outdoor plants can spread their roots far and wide to absorb nutrients from the earth. Houseplants—limited to the soil in their containers—need your help in getting the nutrients they require. Regular applications of a commercial fertilizer specifically formulated for flowering houseplants will help them to thrive. But exercise caution: overfertilizing can be fatal.

The major nutrients that all plants must have are nitrogen, phosphorus and potassium. Every fertilizer label shows three numbers that indicate the percentages of nitrogen, phosphorus and potassium (in that order) found in the product. Since nitrogen may promote foliage growth at the expense of blossom production, fertilizers for flowering houseplants often contain less nitrogen than phosphorus or potassium.

Fertilizers come in two basic forms: slow-release and quick-acting. Slow-release fertilizers are usually solids that come in the form of spikes, tablets and resin-coated beads. They release nutrients into the soil over a period of two to three months. As the name implies, slow-release fertilizers take time to work, but they require fewer applications than their quick-acting counterparts. Always water plants before applying solid fertilizer so that the roots will not be burned by high concentrations of mineral salts.

Quick-acting, or water-soluble, fertilizers generally come in the form of powders or drops that you mix with water before applying. These fertilizers speed nutrients to the plant but must be used often. Read the manufacturer's instructions carefully; if in doubt, use less than the recommended amount. As a general rule, apply water-soluble fertilizer every two to four weeks during the growing season, and not at all when plants are dormant. Most newly purchased plants contain slow-release fertilizer in their growing medium, so wait at least two weeks before adding more.

This miniature cymbidium orchid thrives on bright light, high humidity and monthly feedings with a water-soluble fertilizer.

APPLYING A SOLID, SLOW-RELEASE FERTILIZER

Various slow-release fertilizers are available as tablets, spikes and resin-coated beads. They dissolve slowly into the growing medium once they come into contact with water. As they dissolve, they release a steady supply of nutrients for two to three months. No matter which form you use, be sure to water the plant a day or two prior to application; otherwise, a solid fertilizer may burn the plant's dry roots.

APPLYING A WATER-SOLUBLE FERTILIZER

Soluble fertilizers are available as colored powder and as concentrated liquids. They are dissolved in water before being applied so that the nutrients are quickly absorbed by the plant. Follow the manufacturer's instructions for the rate of application; most products offer a choice between a highly diluted solution that can be applied with each normal watering and a stronger solution that is applied less frequently. □

MIDWINTER COLOR FROM EARLY-BLOOMING BULBS

Few things make a room cheerier during the dim days of winter than a couple of containers full of spring bulbs that are blooming ahead of time. It is not hard to force bulbs to bloom, especially the so-called tender varieties—bulbs native to southerly, temperate regions. Hardy northern flowers such as tulips and daffodils are a bit more difficult, but even they can be coaxed to bloom indoors by Christmastime or shortly thereafter.

The secret of making bulbs grow and flower early is to provide them with springlike conditions. For tender varieties this means simply planting them in shallow bulb pots during the fall and then making sure they get plenty of sun and warmth. A sunny windowsill is ideal, as is a daytime room temperature of 68° to 70° F. How to pot the bulbs and stake them so they stand tall is described opposite and on the following pages.

Exactly when in the fall to do the potting depends on how soon you want the bulbs to bloom—and how long it takes them to do it. Some bulbs, like the handsome, fragrant freesias illustrated here, need three months of growth time before they flower. For Christmas blooms, plant them in late September. Other bulbs require only three weeks or a month to shoot up and blossom. Check the dictionary in this volume for the times required by various species. Check also to determine how deep to plant the bulbs in their pots; depth differs from one species to another.

It is more difficult to force hardy northern bulbs to bloom ahead of time because they must go through a period of winterlike cold before being ready to grow. Most need to be chilled from six to 16 weeks after being planted in pots. This necessary winterizing process, and how and where to do it, is explained in the box on the bottom of page 29.

Two freesias, loosely restrained by wire supports, display their contrasting yellow and lavender blooms. Freesias are propagated from corms that cannot withstand freezing temperatures. They can, however, be forced to bloom indoors at any time of year to make colorful, fragrant houseplants.

1 In preparation for forcing tender spring bulbs to bloom for winter, fill a bulb pan—which is wider and shallower than a standard flowerpot—about half full of a standard soilless growing mixture. Then lay the bulbs on top. In general, use as many bulbs as will fit without touching, and place the larger ones in the center since they will grow taller than the others.

2 Cover the bulbs with more of the growing medium. With freesias, cover them completely so that the tips are about an inch below the surface; other bulbs may need a shallower top layer of growing medium. Firm the soilless mix with your fingers and water thoroughly. Then make a label, giving the name of the species you have potted and the date, so that you will know about when the bulbs should start sending up shoots and how long it should take them to flower.

3 To simulate spring conditions and cause the bulbs to sprout and grow, place the bulb pan in direct sunlight. Keep the growing medium moist, but avoid overwatering.

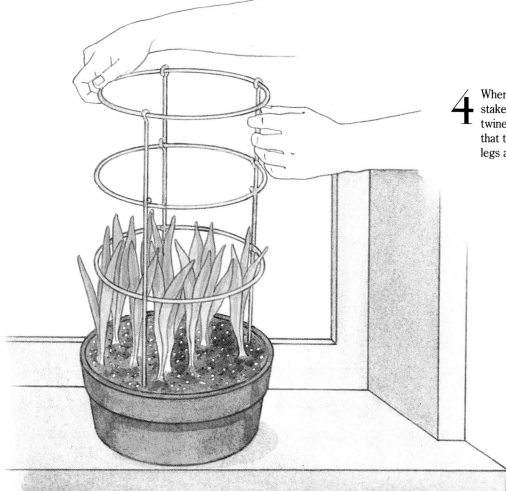

4 When the shoots have grown 4 to 6 inches tall, stake them with ordinary thin bamboo stakes and twine or with a metal bulb stake *(left)*. Make sure that the metal hoops enclose the shoots and that the legs are firmly set in the growing medium.

5 Once the bulbs have grown and flowered, move the pot from direct sun into indirect sunlight. Continue to keep the growing mix moist. Treat the foliage and flowers as you would those of other indoor plants, pinching off dead blooms and removing tired and yellowing foliage. □

SIMULATING WINTER

After being planted in pots, hardy bulbs—hyacinths, crocuses, daffodils, tulips—need cold, wintry conditions before they will grow. Start by watering them thoroughly, letting them drain and wrapping the pots in plastic bags to keep in moisture. Then place the pots in an unheated basement or a garage, where the temperature stays between 35° and 45° F, or in an empty vegetable drawer in the refrigerator. When the chilling period is over and roots have grown, remove the plastic and put the bulbs in a spot that has indirect sunlight and a temperature of about 55° F for several days. Then put them in direct sunlight and generally treat them like the tender bulbs discussed above. They should begin to bloom in one to three weeks.

A REGIMEN FOR WELL-GROOMED PLANTS

Crisp, vividly green foliage handsomely frames a single brilliant reddish orange blossom of a Chinese hibiscus, a tropical plant that thrives indoors. Plants will readily put on such lavish displays when their growing conditions are right and they receive regular grooming and cleaning.

Keeping houseplants trimmed and dust-free ranks in importance with making sure that they have enough water, light and fertilizer. And not just appearance is involved. Plants will not thrive unless their dead or decaying leaves and flowers are snipped off, and the healthy foliage needs to be kept neat as well. The illustrations at right show how best to do this simple but vital pruning, and how leaves should be washed and cleaned.

Keeping foliage free of dust is essential because it is through their leaves that plants take in carbon dioxide and give off oxygen. Even a thin layer of house dust may clog a leaf's pores, or stomata. Worse is the greasy, gritty film left by polluted air. The best cleaning agent for most houseplants is mild soapy water. Do not, however, wash plants whose leaves are coated with downlike hairs; water may spot them. Instead dust the leaves with a small, soft-bristled brush. Commercial foliage cleaners are best avoided; they are supposed to make leaves shine, but frequently they plug up the pores. The same goes for the old-fashioned leaf shiners, oil and milk; they simply attract dirt along with mites and other pests.

When grooming a houseplant, remove all yellowed, dying leaves completely. Besides being unsightly, they deplete a plant's growing energy—and offer targets for insects and diseases. Also cut off all sickly, wilted flowers. This deadheading, as it is called, will encourage plants to produce new blossoms.

For most houseplants, such maintenance should be done once each month or so and more often if you live in a city where grime in the outside air all too readily sifts indoors and into your houseplant garden.

BATHING FOLIAGE

Using mild soapy water and a sponge or a soft cloth, gently wipe off the tops and undersides of all leaves, to make sure their pores are free of grime and dust. Support the leaves with the fingers of your other hand as you do the wiping so that the leaves do not bend or break. For flowering houseplants of the gesneriad family, which have hairy, or so-called pubescent, leaves, use a soft brush to whisk away the dust.

REMOVING SPENT LEAVES

Foliage that looks withered, rotten, burned or discolored should be removed as soon as you notice it. Most leaves will come off if you tug at the base. If not, cut them off with scissors, a sharp knife or pruning shears. For a leaf that is only slightly damaged at the tip, you can trim away the damaged portion, rounding the cut so that it follows the natural shape of the leaf.

DEADHEADING FADED BLOOMS

Once a flower wilts or fades, remove it from the plant—for looks and to encourage new buds. But do not just snip off the old blossom; remove its stem as well, cutting where the small stem joins a larger one. □

CONTROLLING PESTS INDOORS

Indoor plants are less exposed to health-threatening insects and diseases than outdoor plants. Nevertheless, you should keep a lookout for mealybugs, scales, aphids and spider mites. When buying plants, inspect them carefully to make sure they are pest-free. When replanting, use clean pots and sterile growing medium. Keep plants well groomed; promptly remove dead or decaying blossoms and foliage, which can provide a breeding ground for pests.

Regularly examine even healthy-looking plants for insect infestation. Pay special attention to leaf axils, stems and the undersides of leaves. At the first sign of infestation, isolate the plant to keep the trouble from spreading.

The first step to effective treatment is to identify the pest. Mealybugs are small and white, cottonlike in appearance; scales are usually tan, oval-shaped and covered with a hard waxy shell. Both pests weaken plants by sucking sap while excreting a clear sticky substance. To remove mealybugs and scales, rub infested areas with a cotton swab dipped in alcohol. Repeat until all signs of the pests and their eggs are gone.

Aphids are usually green and oval-shaped insects with long legs that feed on plant sap; they cause leaf malformation, yellowing and wilting and can spread diseases. Spider mites, which are microscopic members of the spider family, are no larger than dust specks; the back sides of infested leaves make a rusty red streak when rubbed on white paper. Spider mites get their name from the webs they spin on the plant. Left untreated, these webs can cover the whole plant, which eventually withers and dies. To remove aphids and spider mites, immerse the entire plant in mild soapy water, then rinse with a spray of fresh water. Repeat several times over a period of weeks until the plant is pest-free.

With their dark green leaves and shiny pink blossoms, these Rieger begonias glow with health. To stay that way, they need to be kept free of aphids, spider mites, mealybugs and other pests that prey on houseplants.

MEALYBUGS AND SCALES

White, cottony-looking mealybugs, which congregate along leaf axils, and scales, which are usually found on stems and along leaf petioles and ribs, can be removed by swabbing the infested areas with alcohol-soaked cotton. Be careful not to use excess alcohol as it can damage healthy plant tissue. If the infestation persists, repeat the treatment until all pests are gone.

APHIDS AND SPIDER MITES

Green, oval-shaped aphids, which break the surface of leaves, stems and buds with their beaks and then suck the sap from inside, and spider mites, which betray their presence in the form of fine white webs, can be dislodged from an infested plant by immersing it in a bucket of mild soapy water. Agitate the plant gently, then spray it with fresh water to remove the soap. Repeat if pests reappear. □

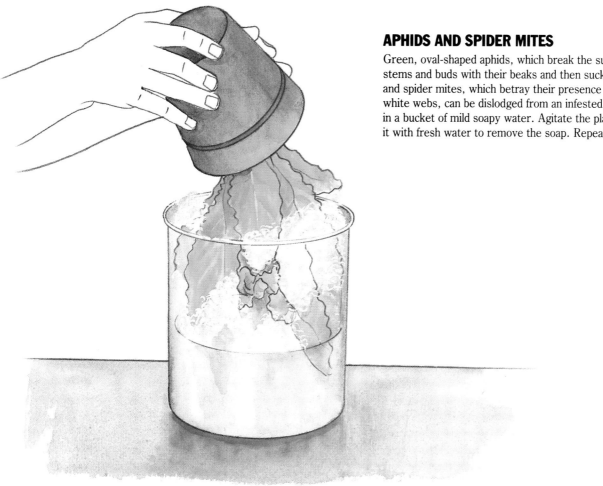

3
NEW PLANTS FROM OLD

S eeing your plants in full bloom may make you wish that you had more of them. Reproducing the ones you have—especially the best blossomers—may be the most successful, and rewarding, route to increasing your collection of flowering houseplants. The following pages show in detail five different methods for propagating flowering houseplants; the method you choose will depend upon both the type of plant you want to reproduce and the result you want. For example, the best way to produce the most offspring from a single plant is by sowing seeds. The new plants may not possess all the characteristics of the parent, but some may be even more colorful and vigorous. If, however, you have a plant that is an especially prolific blossomer, stem or leaf cuttings will produce new plants with the same characteristics as the old. Layering—or burying a stem in an adjacent pot and waiting for it to root—is an equally reliable method of replicating plants with trailing stems. Some plants, such as those with multiple crowns, regularly reproduce themselves without help from anyone. They produce new crowns, and in so doing may outgrow their pots. Dividing them—or separating and repotting the individual crowns—will not only result in new plants, it will invigorate the old ones. For African violet lovers, a section on hybridizing, or producing new varieties by cross-pollination, will enable you to engage your own creativity in the reproductive process.

CROSS-POLLINATION FOR AFRICAN VIOLET HYBRIDS

African violets are among the most popular flowering houseplants for a number of reasons. Their flowers come in many rich, bright colors; their leaves in interesting shapes —flat, ruffled, variegated. And the plants themselves vary in shape and size from large specimens to delicate miniatures to graceful trailing varieties. One or another will fit in any indoor setting. And being tropical in origin—they were first discovered growing in East Africa in 1892—they flourish in the warmth of a sunny window.

But African violets are gratifying to grow for another reason: it is both easy and exciting to make hybrids, creating new plants with unique, never-before-seen blooms. Hybridizing is simple because each African violet flower includes both male and female reproductive organs, as shown in the box on the opposite page. The hybridizing process, described at bottom right and on the next pages, involves little more than taking pollen from the male anther of one African violet and transferring it to the female stigma of another plant. Once fertilized, the ovary will develop a seedpod, which in turn will produce seeds that have a combination of characteristics from the two parent plants.

All this does not happen swiftly. It takes six to nine months for the seedpod to mature, and 12 months more for the seeds to produce a new plant that will flower. But that is part of the excitement for African violet fanciers, waiting to see what the result will be. If the new flowers are exceptionally handsome, you may wish to register your hybrid with the African Violet Society.

The lovely lavender flowers of an African violet clearly display the male anthers, bright yellow with ripe pollen, that are used when hybridizing the plants.

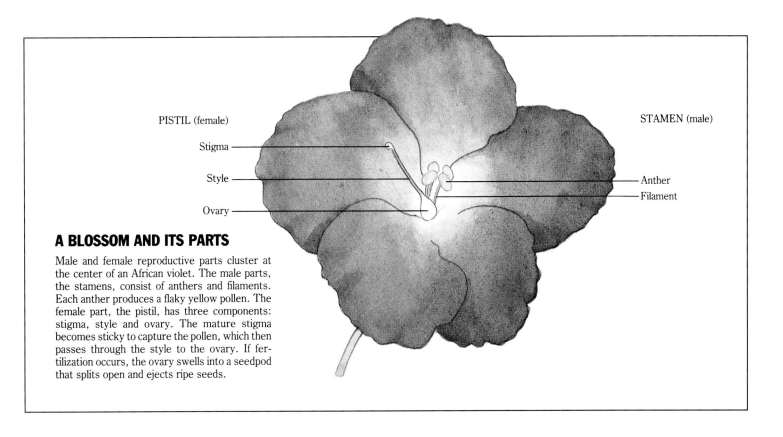

PISTIL (female)   STAMEN (male)

Stigma ——————————————————

Style ——————————————————   —————— Anther
                                                        —————— Filament

Ovary ——————————————

A BLOSSOM AND ITS PARTS

Male and female reproductive parts cluster at the center of an African violet. The male parts, the stamens, consist of anthers and filaments. Each anther produces a flaky yellow pollen. The female part, the pistil, has three components: stigma, style and ovary. The mature stigma becomes sticky to capture the pollen, which then passes through the style to the ovary. If fertilization occurs, the ovary swells into a seedpod that splits open and ejects ripe seeds.

1 To cross or hybridize two African violets, choose one plant to play the part of the male, another to be the female. Make sure that the pollen on the male plant's anthers is ripe, that is, loose and ready to flake off. Then find the stigma in the blossom on the female. It should be slightly sticky so that the pollen will adhere to it.

FEMALE

MALE

2 Remove the stamens from the flowers of the female plant, to keep it from self-pollinating and thus spoiling the hybridization. Use tweezers, small scissors or a small knife blade to break or slice off the stamens while leaving the stigmas intact.

3 With a small, fine-bristled paintbrush or with a pipe cleaner, collect some of the pollen from an anther of the plant serving as the male and brush it gently on a stigma in a flower on the female.

4 Make a **label** that gives the name of the variety to which the **male** African violet belongs, then under it a cross and under that the name of the female variety. Add the date. This will give you a record of what plants you crossed and when. Attach the label to the stem of the female flower just pollinated.

5 If your cross has been successful, a seedpod will develop in a couple of weeks. The pod will gradually turn brown and shrivel over a period of six to nine months. When it is fully dry, remove the flower stalk with the seedpod on it, split the pod and collect the seeds. They can be sown immediately or kept warm and dry in an envelope for up to a year. □

HOUSEPLANTS FROM SEEDS TO SEEDLINGS

Many flowering houseplants can be propagated from seed. Given proper amounts of water, light and warmth, seeds germinate within a few weeks. Of course, some plants are easier to propagate by this method than others; for specific recommendations, consult the Dictionary of Houseplants *(pages 72-137).*

Seeds come in a variety of shapes and sizes; a few, like the seeds of the begonia and those of the gesneriad family, are as fine as dust, but most are big enough to handle singly. Optimum growing conditions vary with the size and type of seed; the instructions printed on seed packets will tell you how far apart to sow the seeds, how deeply to bury them and so on.

Virtually any kind of container can serve as an "incubator" as long as it is clean and shallow and has at least one drainage hole. Options include clay and plastic pots, peat pellets, plastic seed flats, even cutoff milk cartons and plastic salad trays with holes punched in the bottoms.

Immediately after sowing the seeds in a soilless growing medium *(pages 8-9),* place the container in a tray of water until the surface of the growing medium is moist to the touch. Remove from water, allow excess water to drain and transfer the container to a warm place (60° to 80° F) with filtered light. If natural light is unavailable, fluorescent lamps can be used. Move the container into a bright area when the first leaves (called seed leaves) appear.

Keep the growing medium warm and moist throughout the germination period. An easy way to maintain sufficient humidity is to cover the container with a piece of clear plastic; the plastic should trap enough moisture inside to eliminate the need for constant watering.

When at least one set of true leaves (known as foliage leaves) has succeeded the seed leaves, the seedling is ready to be transplanted to a new pot and treated like a mature plant.

Browallia seedlings, transplanted into individual pots, establish themselves in bright, warm sunlight. The maturing plants should blossom in the summer and fall.

1 Select a shallow container with at least one drainage hole; if you use a large plastic tray, punch a few extra holes in the bottom. Fill the container with sterile, soilless growing medium up to ¾ inch from the top. With a plant label, scratch parallel rows of shallow indentations on the surface, leaving at least 1 inch between rows.

2 Sprinkle seeds evenly along the rows *(left)*, following the guidelines for correct spacing printed on the seed packet. To prevent the seeds from drying out, cover the rows with a fine layer of medium.

3 Set the container in a tray of water until the surface of the growing medium feels moist. Then cover the container with a sheet of clear plastic or a plastic bag to retain moisture *(right)*. Then place the covered container in a warm area with filtered light.

4 Once the seeds have germinated, thin out the rows, removing the weakest seedlings to make more room for the strongest. When the seedlings have grown at least one pair of true leaves, gently lift them one by one from the container with a spoon *(left)* or with a plant label. If it is necessary to handle them, hold the seedlings by their leaves, not by their tender stems.

5 Have ready a new pot filled with sterile, soilless growing medium. Poke a hole in the surface with your finger; lower the seedling into the hole and gently firm the medium around the stem. Transplant all other seedlings in the same manner, taking special care not to touch the stems. □

DIVIDING PLANTS THAT HAVE MULTIPLE CROWNS

One of the easiest ways to multiply your stock of houseplants is to take advantage of their propensity for asexual reproduction by means of division. Under the proper conditions, when a piece of a plant is separated from the parent, it takes root and begins to grow independently. Among the flowering houseplants that can be divided successfully are African violets, begonias, kaffir lilies and most bromeliads. But almost any plant can be divided if it forms multiple crowns. A crown is a clump of foliage, usually arranged in the shape of a rosette, that emerges from a central point at the base of the plant.

Once you have selected a plant for division, remove it from its container. With a sharp knife separate one or more crowns from the parent plant. Make your cut between the tops of two crowns and down through the root ball.

In order to survive on its own, each division must have some healthy top growth and a sizable root system to support it. If the root area of a division is considerably smaller than the top growth, cut off some foliage; it will grow back after replanting.

Repot the divisions immediately in an appropriate growing medium. Water them thoroughly and place them where the light is bright but indirect. Once new shoots appear, you can transplant each division to its permanent location and treat it as a mature plant.

The kaffir lily, which flowers in late winter and early spring, is easily propagated by dividing its roots soon after the plant has blossomed.

1 To divide a plant for propagation, first carefully remove the parent plant from its container *(below)*. Remove some of the growing medium from the root ball so that you can more easily distinguish the individual crowns.

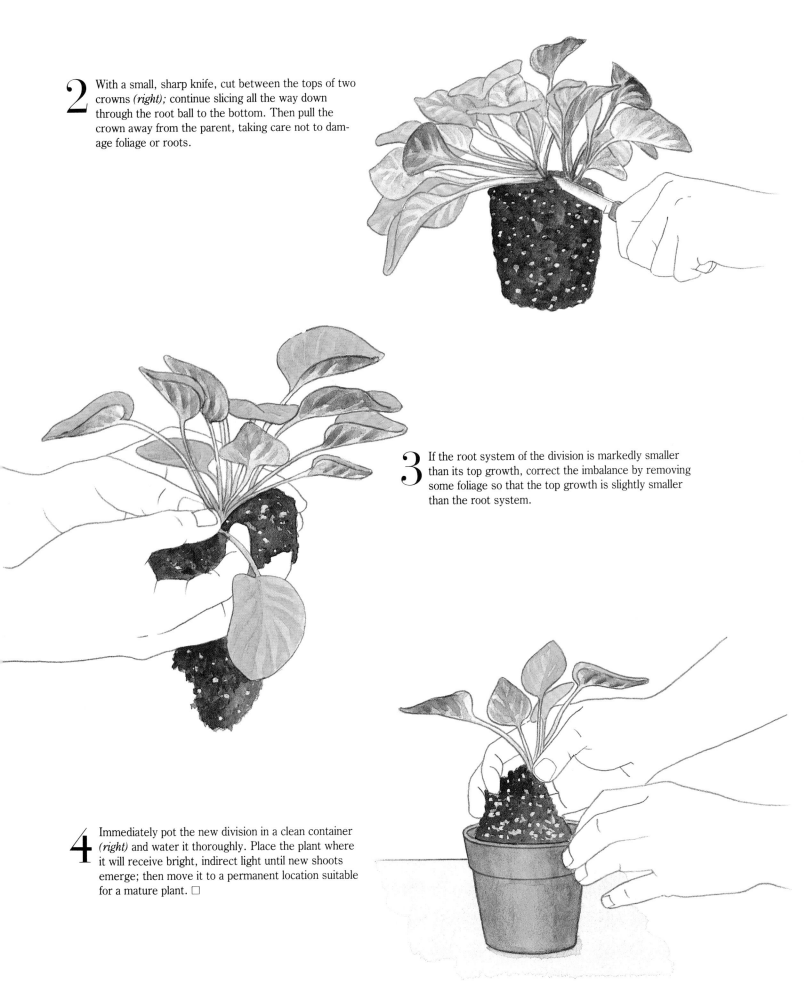

2 With a small, sharp knife, cut between the tops of two crowns *(right);* continue slicing all the way down through the root ball to the bottom. Then pull the crown away from the parent, taking care not to damage foliage or roots.

3 If the root system of the division is markedly smaller than its top growth, correct the imbalance by removing some foliage so that the top growth is slightly smaller than the root system.

4 Immediately pot the new division in a clean container *(right)* and water it thoroughly. Place the plant where it will receive bright, indirect light until new shoots emerge; then move it to a permanent location suitable for a mature plant. □

NEW PLANTS
FROM STEM AND LEAF CUTTINGS

Any houseplant that has nonwoody stems—and most houseplants do—can be reproduced from stem cuttings. The few houseplants that have thick, fleshy leaves—African violets and begonias—can be reproduced by means of leaf cuttings. Either kind of cutting will send out new shoots that will signal the beginning of a new plant.

A stem cutting must include at least one node—the place where a leaf diverges from the stem; it is from the node that the new roots will develop. There are two kinds of stem cuttings. One is a tip cutting, which, as the name implies, is taken from the tip of the stem. To make one, cut just below a node that lies anywhere from 4 to 6 inches from the tip. Remove all flowers and flower buds, strip foliage from the lower third of the cutting, dip the cut end in rooting hormone powder, and insert it 1 to 2 inches deep in soilless medium, or straight vermiculite or perlite.

The other kind of stem cutting is a medial cutting—one taken from somewhere between the tip and the base of the stem. If the stem is long enough, you can take several of these after first removing the tip. Each medial cutting should include two nodes; make one cut just above a node and the other cut just below a second node. Remove flowers and foliage as with a tip cutting and insert the lower end 1 to 2 inches deep in rooting medium.

While rooting, all cuttings need sufficient warmth, moisture and bright indirect light. The best way to ensure optimal conditions is to create a minigreenhouse by enclosing the cutting in a glass dome or a plastic bag.

To check on the growth of the root system, gently tug on each cutting after 10 days to three weeks; once it has developed roots, the cutting will resist being pulled out. If the roots are 1 inch long, carefully lift the cutting from the medium and transplant it to a permanent container.

For propagation by leaf cutting, see the box on page 47.

The soft but sturdy stems of this glory bush provide ideal material for cloning—reliable reproduction of the parent plant through stem cuttings.

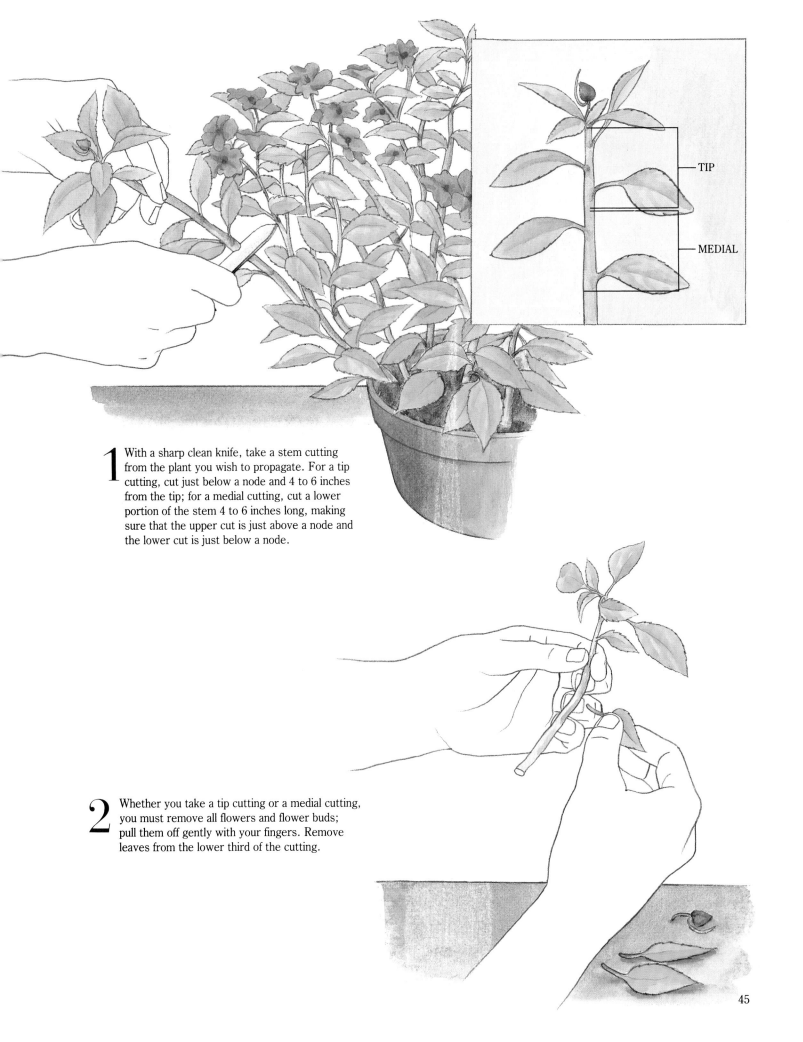

TIP

MEDIAL

1 With a sharp clean knife, take a stem cutting from the plant you wish to propagate. For a tip cutting, cut just below a node and 4 to 6 inches from the tip; for a medial cutting, cut a lower portion of the stem 4 to 6 inches long, making sure that the upper cut is just above a node and the lower cut is just below a node.

2 Whether you take a tip cutting or a medial cutting, you must remove all flowers and flower buds; pull them off gently with your fingers. Remove leaves from the lower third of the cutting.

3 To stimulate root development, dust the bottom end of the cutting with rooting hormone powder that has been spread on a paper towel.

4 Use a stick to poke a hole 1 to 2 inches deep in the rooting medium. Insert the cutting and firm the medium around the stem. If you are taking multiple cuttings from a plant, you can root several in one pot. Water thoroughly.

5 Enclose the cutting in a minigreenhouse—a glass dome or a plastic bag supported by two or more sticks—while the roots develop. Place the pot in bright indirect sunlight (direct sun could cause a damaging buildup of heat inside the minigreenhouse). Check for new roots from time to time; when they have grown to be about 1 inch long, transplant the cutting to a fresh pot and treat it as an adult plant. □

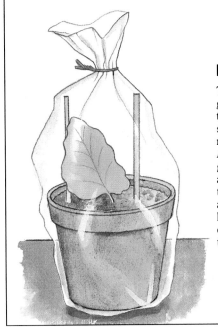

ROOTING A LEAF CUTTING

To propagate African violets and some begonias, select a healthy, mature leaf with a stalk that is 1 to 2 inches long. Insert the base of the stalk, at a 45° angle, into a standard rooting medium to a depth of 1 inch. Water thoroughly. As with stem cuttings, enclose the pot in a minigreenhouse and place it in bright indirect light. In a few weeks, a shoot will develop at the base of the parent leaf. When the plantlet is about 1 inch across and well formed, remove the minigreenhouse and cut off the parent leaf at its base and discard it. Let the plantlet continue to grow in the same pot.

LAYERING: PROPAGATING FROM STEMS THAT ROOT THEMSELVES

The limber stems of a miniature wax plant—here supported by a trellis—lend themselves readily to propagation by layering.

Some flowering houseplants make propagation easy for the home gardener. Among the easiest of all are plants that put out trailing stems—because these stems have a natural propensity to develop roots whenever they are brought into contact with a growing medium. All you have to do is bare a small portion of flexible stem, bury it (while it is still attached to the parent plant) in a separate pot of growing medium, secure the buried portion in place and wait. This simple procedure, known as layering, is highly reliable since it takes advantage of one of the plant's own mechanisms for self-reproduction. One advantage of propagation by layering is that you can root several stems from the same plant at the same time. Bury each stem in its own pot of growing medium.

Depending on the type of plant, roots will start growing from a layered stem within one to four months. During this time the parent plant and the stem should be disturbed as little as possible. For best results, pin the stem to the surface of the growing medium with a U-shaped piece of wire. Use a standard soilless medium, and make sure to keep the medium moist.

After a month or so, check the layered stem to see if any roots have developed. Pull gently with your fingers; if you feel resistance, the roots are ready to support an independent plant. Sever the rooted stem from the parent; take care not to dislodge it from the growing medium. The new plant should thrive in its own pot, and the parent will be none the worse for the layering treatment.

Plants that are especially suitable for layering include flame violet, strawberry geranium, pomegranate and black-eyed Susan vine.

1 For propagating a plant by layering, choose one with a long trailing stem. Remove the leaves from a portion of the stem behind the growing tip. Place a freshly filled pot of soilless growing medium alongside the parent and bury the bare portion of the stem just below the surface of the medium.

2 To ensure that the layered stem remains in contact with the growing medium at all times, secure it with a piece of wire bent into a U shape *(left)*. Push the wire into the medium until it just touches the buried portion, taking care not to cut or bruise the stem. Keep the growing medium moist while the stem is rooting.

3 After a month or so, pull gently on the buried stem to see if it has developed roots. When the stem has rooted sufficiently to resist your pull, sever it from the parent with a clean knife or shears; cut between the rooted portion and the parent *(right)*. Let the new plant continue to grow in its own pot. □

4
HOUSEPLANTS ON DISPLAY

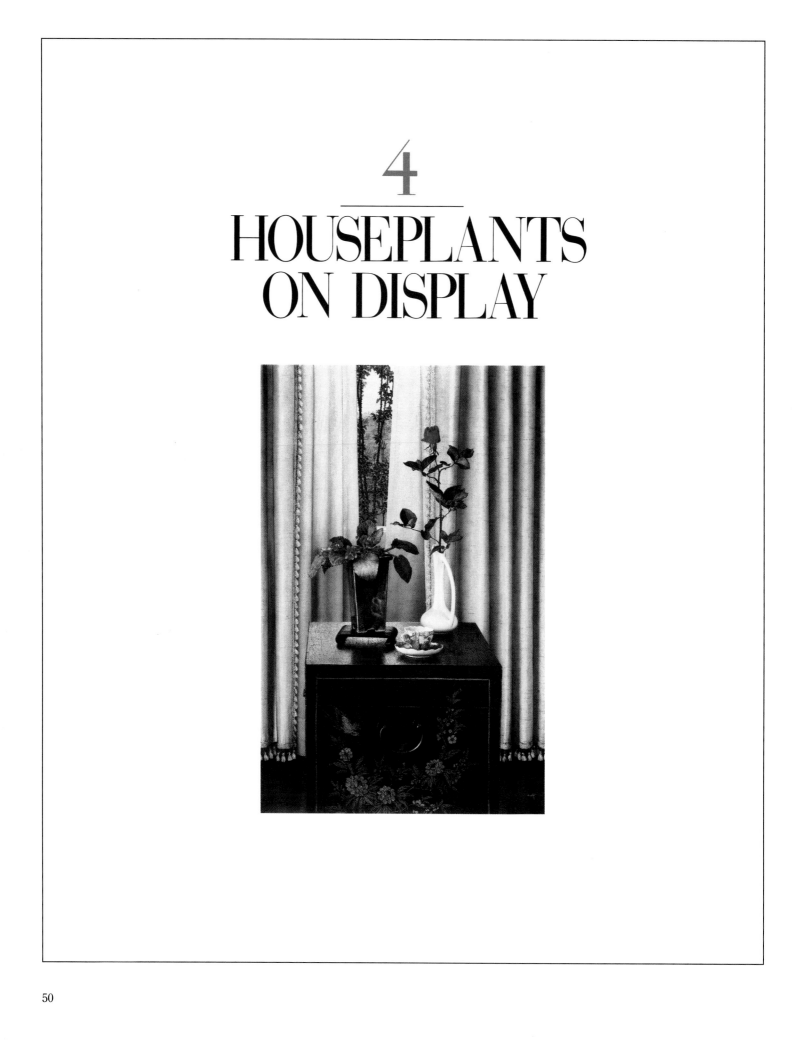

Exhibiting plants in a show is not just for commercial growers. Nearly every show sponsors awards in amateur categories too. And although some participants may view the competition as the focus of the event, a show offers much more than that to hobbyists; it provides an opportunity for growers of flowering plants to share their common interests, their knowledge and their enthusiasm.

Orchids and African violets are among the most widely exhibited plants—perhaps because of their exquisite beauty, perhaps because they offer so many varieties and so many possibilities for new hybrids and colors. Contained in the pages that follow are suggestions that will help you not only to grow these two types of plants for show, but also to grow especially healthy and beautiful plants, even if they are never displayed outside your living room. Separate sections on how to train African violets *(pages 52-53)* and orchids *(pages 54-55)* reveal the secrets of cultivating show-worthy plants. Suggestions on the best way to clean these delicate exotics can be found on pages 56-57. Additional advice on transporting plants without damaging them is useful whether they are being taken to a show or to a friend's house as a gift. Finally, detailed information on what judges look for in plants that are grown for show *(pages 58-61)* will help you to prepare for such events by giving you an idea of how these flowering plants look when they are at their best.

TRAINING
AN AFRICAN VIOLET

Raising an African violet for show requires the usual good care you would give any valued houseplant: the right growing medium, water, light, fertilizer *(Chapter 1)*. But show judges have quite specific ideas about how blooms and leaves should look, and how they should combine to produce a compact overall appearance. It often takes some early training to get even the healthiest and most promising young plant into show-worthy shape.

The first requirement is that the leaves grow symmetrically, forming a near circle as shown opposite *(Step 2)*. They should also overlap one another so that their stalks and the growing medium beneath are hidden. Further, the leaves ought to grow on an even horizontal plane. As for the flowers, they need to be in peak bloom at show time.

All this can be encouraged with a little gentle manipulation. Starting when the plant is young, make sure that it is in the center of its pot and gets light evenly on all sides. Remove any leaves that spoil the symmetry by shooting off in odd directions. And pluck out any new crowns—clusters of tiny leaves—that emerge from the base of the plant.

To move a leaf over and fill in a gap, prop it in place with a toothpick. After a few weeks the leaf should be growing in the right spot on its own. For leaves that droop over the rim of the pot, you can use a paper collar *(opposite)* to lift them up and promote horizontal growth.

To make your plant bloom luxuriantly, disbud it—taking off nascent blooms up to a few months before the show. Then the plant will flower into a mass of blossoms in time for the exhibition.

An African violet of the variety 'Coral Kiss' exhibits a tight central cluster of blossoms and overlapping leaves—all qualities of a show-worthy plant.

1 To begin readying an African violet for showing, train the leaves to grow symmetrically by cutting off any rangy, independent ones with a knife or scissors. Also be sure you have only one plant by snipping off any extra crowns you see emerging from the plant's base.

2 If the remaining leaves are growing unevenly, leaving gaps between them *(above, left)*, push as many as necessary into the proper position, and anchor them with toothpicks pressed into the growing medium, until the entire leaf arrangement approaches the symmetrical ideal *(above, right)*.

3 For leaves that have begun to droop over the rim of the pot, make a collar out of a plastic-coated paper plate. Cut a hole in the center of the plate about half the diameter of the pot. Slit the plate from the center hole to the rim for easy adjustment to the pot.

4 Slip the collar up the side of the pot until it rests under the foliage and on top of the pot's rim. Leave the collar in place for several weeks, to train the leaves to grow in a horizontal plane.

5 To make sure your African violet is in full bloom when time for a flower show arrives, remove the buds regularly until eight or 10 weeks before the exhibition. Break off the new buds with your fingers or snip them off with a small pair of scissors. Be sure you get the entire bud and its stem. □

STAKES
TO MAKE ORCHIDS STAND STRAIGHT

Orchids grown for exhibition at flower shows do not require elaborate training. Having a blue-ribbon plant depends rather on good growing conditions, good care—and some genetic luck. But show orchids do need to be staked, to keep their long flower stems from bending and flopping over. Obviously, orchids that stand up so their lovely blossoms can be seen and appreciated are going to be better for showing, and that is how the people who run flower shows want them exhibited.

The way orchids are staked depends on their growing habits. Some orchids, such as dendrobium and cattleya, have several good-sized stems called pseudobulbs. The newest bears this year's flower; the others represent stems that have finished flowering. All the pseudobulbs need to be staked to keep the plants from looking unkempt. It is best to use two supports, as shown in the drawings of a cattleya being staked on the opposite page, one of stiff bamboo for the mature pseudobulbs that have finished flowering, another, of wire, for the new stem that is about to flower.

Other orchids do not need double staking. Butterfly orchids, for example, produce several pseudobulbs, but the pseudobulbs are low-growing and do not become top-heavy and troublesome. The moth orchid *(box, opposite)* is similar, producing a few small leaves to go with the plant's long, slim, flower-topped stem. With these orchids, only the tall flower stalk requires staking. A single thin wire will suffice to hold aloft the plants' gorgeous blooms.

Their bright blooms and crisp foliage guided upward by staking, two cattleyas claim prize ribbons at an orchid society show.

1 Begin staking a cattleya or similar orchid when its leafy stems, or pseudobulbs, begin to lean beyond the rim of the pot. For best results, use a bamboo stake that is thin enough to be inconspicuous but strong enough to support the heavy stems. Set the stake firmly near the middle of the pot.

2 Gently pull each pseudobulb upward and tie it to the stake with a bit of raffia or soft green twine. Make sure the ties are securely attached to the stake but looped loosely like a sling around the pseudobulbs.

3 When the orchid has produced a pseudobulb with flower buds, place a second stake near the center of the pot. Carefully straighten the flower stem and, again using raffia or string, secure the stem to the stake just below the flower buds. This stake should be a length of fairly stiff 11-gauge wire, strong enough to support the stem as its buds blossom into flowers. □

SUPPORT FOR A SLENDER STEM

Orchids that have tall, thin stems with flowering spikes on top but a minimum of lower growth, such as the moth orchid shown at right, need only single supports of light, 16-gauge corsage wire to keep their blooms upright. Staking should be done just before the flower buds emerge; it helps to study the growth pattern of your orchid and be able to estimate how tall the spike will be when the buds appear. To do the staking, merely cut a piece of wire to the proper length and insert one end in the center of the pot. Then, holding the stem upright, loop the other end of the wire around it near the top.

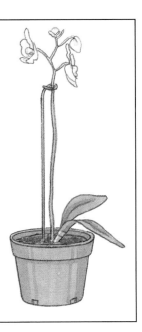

GETTING PLANTS READY TO GO TO A SHOW

Once houseplants have been nurtured into show-worthy shape *(pages 52-55),* they still need some last-minute sprucing up so they will look their best. They also need to be packed so that no damage occurs on the way to the show itself. The drawings on this and the opposite page demonstrate how to prepare and transport a show-bound African violet; most of the steps can be used for show orchids as well, and for other houseplants.

The grooming should be done the day before the show. Remove any wilting flowers and tired foliage with your fingers or scissors, and do a careful check for any hidden insects. Then wash the healthy foliage. For most houseplants, orchids included, mild soapy water applied with a soft cloth or a sponge is best *(pages 30-31).* African violets, though, are different. Normally their pubescent leaves should be kept dry, but a plant that is about to be shown needs to have its foliage rinsed with plain water—tepid water to avoid spotting the leaves. A paper collar can be used to prevent the growing medium from getting wet and spattering the foliage.

On the day of the show, pack your plant (or plants) so that the pot contents will not spill and so that leaves and flowers do not rub against each other or anything else. You can put a pot in a box and pack crumpled newspaper around it or, better, convert the box into a pot holder as shown at far right. Whatever method you employ, be sure the box does not slide about the car as you drive to the show, and that the plants are not exposed to excessive heat or cold in transit.

All set for a trip to a show, four miniature African violets rest securely in a box-within-a-box. The plants are kept upright by being placed in holes cut into the bottom of an inverted box. That box is then set inside another to give the plants additional protection.

1 To wash the foliage of an African violet you intend to show, place a paper collar *(pages 52-53)* around the plant underneath the foliage, then rinse the leaves with tepid water. After washing, shake the plant to remove excess moisture and put it in a warm, bright spot to dry—but not in direct sunlight, which may discolor the leaves.

2 For the ideal pot carrier, turn a cardboard box upside down and cut a hole in the bottom. The hole should be slightly larger than the circumference of the bottom of the pot. If you are taking more than one plant to the show, cut more holes—but make them far enough apart so that the plants' foliage and flowers do not come in contact with each other.

3 Fit each pot in a hole so that it stands securely in position, then set the box in your car, preferably on the floor or the front seat where it will not slide around. In summer, open the car windows for some air—but not so wide that the wind will blow off leaves or flowers. In winter, use the heater to keep the plant warm. Also, shade your plants from sun coming in the car windows with a piece of old sheet or a screen of tissue paper.

4 When you have arrived at the show, do a last bit of grooming and cleaning. Whisk any dust from the leaves with a small, soft-bristled paintbrush. Remove any leaves or flowers that have begun to wilt during the trip, or have somehow gotten damaged in transit. And save your special carrying box, to protect your plants on the way home. □

WHAT JUDGES LOOK FOR
IN AFRICAN VIOLETS

African violets of several varieties display their prize ribbons at a plant show. Although the colors and shapes of their blossoms differ from one plant to another, these show violets share some important characteristics: large, profuse blooms that are rich in color and leaves that are arranged symmetrically.

Once you and your plant have arrived at the flower show, you will need to register and—after giving your entry a last grooming —fill out a label identifying the variety you are exhibiting. Your plant will then be put on a table among other entries of the same general type; if it is an African violet, the types will be standards, semi-miniatures, miniatures, trailing plants and new varieties. Within each section, the plants will probably be arranged in subgroups according to flower color. Then the judges will begin looking, comparing, evaluating.

What the judges will be looking for is shown on the opposite page. Essentially, a prizewinning specimen has to excel in five categories. The first is symmetry, or the overall shape of the plant. The emphasis here is on the leaves, which should be evenly spaced and form a green rosette around the central blooms. The second category is health and general condition. Clearly the judges will prefer a vibrantly healthy plant to one that seems a shade past its prime. Then they will look at the number of blooms, the size of the individual flowers and the richness or brilliance of their color.

For convenience, flower show judges use a point system. The total almost invariably is 100 with a maximum of 25 points each awarded for symmetry, condition and number of flowers, 15 points for size of blooms and 10 for their color. It is, of course, the plants gaining the highest point totals that get the blue ribbons or other awards—and are placed on an award table for everyone to admire.

A last note about showing: be sure to get hold of a copy of a show's rules ahead of time. They often, for example, stipulate that you can enter only one plant of any given variety, that flare-top pots are not allowed and that African violets must have their pots covered in aluminum foil "dull side out." There is no use getting to an exhibition and finding your plant, for some rules infraction, cannot be shown.

SIZE AND TYPE OF BLOOM

Excellence here depends on the variety of the plant being shown, since blooms differ from one type of African violet to another. Generally, though, the flowers ought to be large for their type and have the correct number of petals.

CONDITION

Good grooming and excellent maintenance count heavily. The plant should have no damaged leaves or spent flowers, and no dust on the foliage. All props such as toothpicks used to train the growth need to be removed.

ABUNDANCE OF BLOOMS

Number of flowers counts, so plants should be shown when they are at the peak of bloom. As a rule of thumb, a standard African violet, when in full bloom, such as the one shown here, should have about 20 blossoms.

SYMMETRY

The leaves of an African violet should in effect form a green halo around the blossoms. For most varieties, the leaves in each row should overlap so that there are no gaps, and each row should evenly overlap the row beneath it.

COLOR OF BLOSSOMS

The colors of an African violet's flowers should be characteristic of its variety; a plant that normally produces bicolored blossoms should not have any solid-colored ones, and in types producing single-hued blooms, the flower color should be bright, strong and clear. □

WHAT JUDGES LOOK FOR IN SHOW ORCHIDS

A hybrid cattleya orchid produces three gorgeous and nearly identical blossoms, all with rich orange petals and with the deeper-colored lips that are a mark of a show-quality plant.

Getting an orchid ready for a flower show calls for most of the same preparations used when showing an African violet *(pages 52-53)*. The plant must be in the best possible shape: clean, dust-free and with all less-than-healthy leaves and pseudobulbs snipped off—and in full bloom. An orchid should be staked to show off its flowers *(pages 54-55)*, but the staking ought to be unobtrusive.

At the show, you will need to label your entry following the instructions issued by the show's sponsors. They will want to know the plant variety—cattleya, dendrobium, cymbidium or whatever—and other information as well, including the names of the parent plants if yours is a hybrid. The sponsors will organize the entries into classes according to types of exhibitors: novices, hobbyists, commercial growers, those showing cut flower arrangements and so on.

What is different about orchid shows is that the judges look almost exclusively at the quality of the plant's blossoms. The rest of the plant should look clean and vigorous, but the flower is what really counts. It should be full and symmetrical, and its various parts— three sepals (an upper, or dorsal, one and two lateral ones), the petals, the lip—should be properly shaped and in proportion to one another, as shown in the cattleya pictured opposite. Judges also give high marks to flowers that have clear, bright color, fine texture and larger-than-usual size for their variety.

The judges use a point scale when making their evaluations. Of a total of 100 points, they award a maximum of 30 for blossom shape, another 30 for color. The remaining 40 points are for other qualities: size of blooms, their substance and texture—and the vigor of the stem holding them up. Because so much emphasis is devoted to the form of a blossom—and so many points ride on it—any flower that shows signs of having been manipulated into its present shape is disqualified from competition.

FLOWER COLOR

The blossoms should have a clear, bright and even color throughout its sepals and its petals. In general, the hue ought to be characteristic of the variety of orchid—although judges will give high marks to a flower of an unusual shade if the color is strong and not randomly splashed with other hues. The lip should be of a still richer color that complements that of petals and sepals.

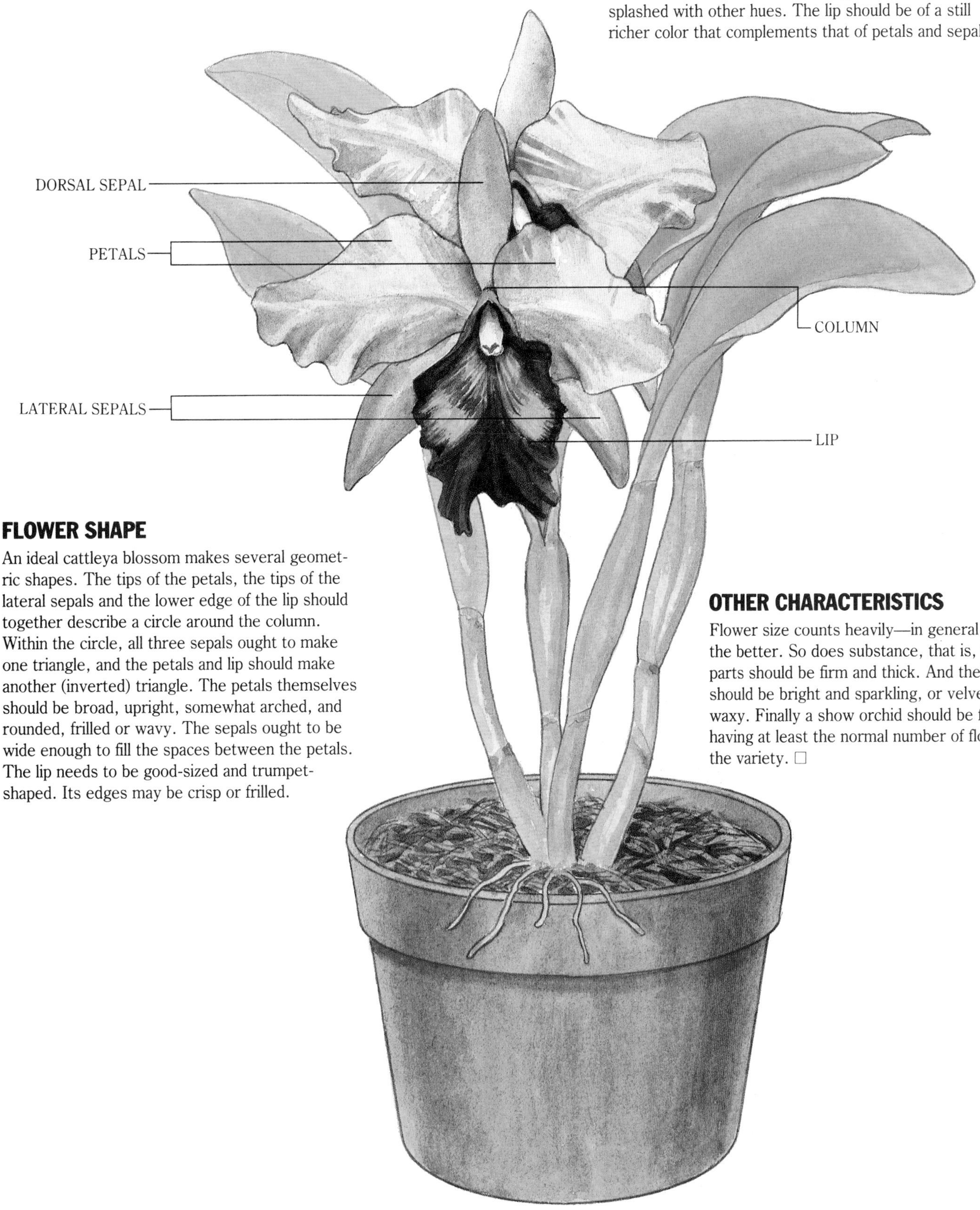

DORSAL SEPAL

PETALS

COLUMN

LATERAL SEPALS

LIP

FLOWER SHAPE

An ideal cattleya blossom makes several geometric shapes. The tips of the petals, the tips of the lateral sepals and the lower edge of the lip should together describe a circle around the column. Within the circle, all three sepals ought to make one triangle, and the petals and lip should make another (inverted) triangle. The petals themselves should be broad, upright, somewhat arched, and rounded, frilled or wavy. The sepals ought to be wide enough to fill the spaces between the petals. The lip needs to be good-sized and trumpet-shaped. Its edges may be crisp or frilled.

OTHER CHARACTERISTICS

Flower size counts heavily—in general, the bigger the better. So does substance, that is, the flower parts should be firm and thick. And their texture should be bright and sparkling, or velvety or waxy. Finally a show orchid should be floriferous, having at least the normal number of flowers for the variety. □

5
WORKING IN TANDEM WITH NATURE

Although indoor plants are protected from the elements, they nevertheless respond to changes of season. Blossoming plants are especially sensitive to changes in temperature and light. Keeping them healthy demands an awareness of their seasonal needs; in winter, for example, some need to go dormant, others need supplemental light and still others need to be placed in a cool corner of the room to bring on their blossoms. The following pages provide a guide to seasonal maintenance for specific flowering species, as well as general advice on when it is best to take cuttings or repot and divide plants.

In addition to their seasonal needs, flowering houseplants occasionally demand emergency attention. A section entitled "What to Do When Things Go Wrong" will help you to diagnose attacks by insects and diseases, to cure them and to prevent them from recurring. There is additional information on recognizing the symptoms of over- and under-watering and too much and too little light—problems specific to plants that spend their lives indoors.

A final section, entitled "Tips and Techniques," contains advice on how to get the most out of your plants. Information on what to look for—and what to avoid—when purchasing plants will help you to start off with the healthiest plants possible. Hints on arranging plants, as well as suggestions for growing fragrant species, are intended to add to the pleasures that flowering houseplants bring.

A CHECKLIST FOR MAINTENANCE SEASON BY SEASON

WINTER

- Move bulbs that have been chilled outdoors back into the house for forcing.
- Store dormant blood lily bulbs.
- Plant gloriosa lily and ornithogalum bulbs and resume normal care.
- Cut back coralberry and Cape leadwort before new growth starts.
- Cut back camellia and daphne after the flowers fade.
- Allow bougainvillea to go dormant.
- Place miniature roses, African violets and geraniums under fluorescent lights; they do not need to go dormant in winter and they benefit from supplemental light when days are short. Water and fertilize regularly.
- Decrease watering and discontinue fertilizing flowering houseplants that do not receive supplemental light.
- Protect plants from cold drafts.
- Place plants in pebble trays or use a humidifier to counteract the drying effects of indoor heating.
- Inspect flowering houseplants for signs of insects and diseases, especially spider mites, which thrive in winter.
- Order seeds for spring sowing.
- Clean empty pots and prepare growing medium for spring repotting and propagation.

SPRING

- Cut back flowering maple, chenille plant, allamanda, zebra plant, coffee plant, crown-of-thorns, scarlet plume, Chinese hibiscus, shrimp plant, Brazilian plume flower and pomegranate before new growth starts.
- Cut back brunfelsia, camellia, orchid cactus, poinsettia and azalea after flowers fade; cut back Jerusalem cherry after berries fall.
- Move chrysanthemum, azalea and primrose into the garden after the flowers fade.
- Start watering dormant blood lily bulbs.
- Store dormant Guernsey lily until midsummer.
- Divide bulbs of spider lily and rhizomes of magic flower and repot. Divide kaffir lily after flowers fade.
- Allow cyclamen to go dormant.
- Check to see whether plants are pot-bound and repot if necessary.
- Increase watering and start or increase fertilizing as days lengthen and flowering houseplants resume active growth.
- Sow seeds, and take stem and leaf cuttings to propagate flowering houseplants. Divide and repot plants that require thinning.
- Pinch back new growth to keep plants bushy.

SUMMER

- Cut back basket plant, glory bower, goldfish plant, carpet plant, flame-of-the-woods, oleander, mandevilla and Egyptian star after flowers fade.

- Subject kalanchoe to darkness 14 hours a night for six weeks to force it to bloom.

- Allow lycoris to go dormant in early summer; start rewatering in late summer.

- Take Guernsey lily out of storage and water.

- Place agapanthus, camellia, cattleya, cymbidium, dendrobium, poinsettia, fuchsia, Jerusalem cherry and jasmine in a sheltered spot outdoors and water as needed.

- Allow amaryllis, oxalis and freesia to go dormant and store in a cool spot.

- Place Thanksgiving cactus in a cool room in mid-August and subject it to 12 hours of darkness a night for eight weeks so it will bloom for the holiday.

- Sow ornamental pepper seeds for winter holiday fruit; sow pocketbook plant and browallia seeds.

- Look carefully at plants located near windows. If the foliage becomes bleached or if the edges of leaves and petals start to burn, move the plants away from the window.

- Transplant seedlings and cuttings started in spring into individual pots.

- Continue to water and fertilize summer-flowering plants regularly.

- Inspect flowering houseplants for signs of insects and diseases.

FALL

- Cut back bougainvillea, heliotrope, black-eyed Susan vine, lantana, fuchsia and passionflower after the flowers fade.

- Subject poinsettia to darkness 15 hours a night for six weeks beginning in mid-September so it will bloom at Christmastime. Place Christmas cactus in a cool room and subject it to darkness 16 hours a night for four weeks to force it to blossom for Christmas.

- Pot crocus, hyacinth, iris, lily, grape hyacinth, daffodils, squill and tulips and subject them to cold treatment for forcing.

- Chill azalea and hydrangea to force them to set flower buds.

- Retrieve oxalis and amaryllis plants from storage and resume normal care.

- Divide and repot cyclamen and freesia.

- Allow gloriosa lily to go dormant.

- Store gloxinia tubers for two to four months, repot and return to the house.

- Root citrus cuttings.

- Withhold water from magic flower until the foliage wilts and dies, so that you force the plant to go dormant; then store it until spring.

- Wash the pots and the foliage of plants that spent the summer outdoors to rid them of insects and diseases, and then bring them back into the house. Also check inside pots for insects that may have crawled through drainage holes.

- Reduce watering and fertilizing as days grow shorter.

- Inspect flowering houseplants for signs of insects and diseases.

WHAT TO DO
WHEN THINGS GO WRONG

PROBLEM	CAUSE	SOLUTION
Plant growth is stunted and leaves turn yellow, become deformed and fall. White, fluffy masses appear where leaves join stems and on the undersides of leaves. Leaves may be covered with a sticky substance on which a black, sooty mold may grow.	Mealybugs, oval insects that are up to ¼ inch long and covered with a white, cottony wax. They suck plant juices and excrete a shiny substance called honeydew on which black fungi grow.	If the infestation is small, insects may be picked off by hand or killed by dabbing them with a cotton swab dipped in rubbing alcohol. Wash the foliage with warm water after treatment. If the infestation is severe, use an insecticidal soap or a chemical insecticide.
Plant growth is stunted and leaves wilt and may turn yellow, especially on hot days. Leaves may also become thick and blistered. Removing plants from their pots reveals short, thick roots with irregular swellings.	Root knot nematodes, sometimes called eelworms, which are nearly microscopic, wormlike insects.	Discard infested plants and their growing medium. There are no chemical controls for root knot nematodes. When potting new plants, do not use garden soil in the potting mix.
Plants become stunted and leaves turn yellow, wilt and die. Stems and leaves are often covered with a sticky or waxy film. Small brown, green, gray or white lumps appear on the stems and on the undersides of the leaves.	Scales, flat, oval or rounded insects that are up to ¼ inch long. They suck plant juices and secrete a waxy or sticky film.	If the infestation is small, remove scales by hand or with a small brush. Wash the leaves with soapy water and rinse, or dab the insects with alcohol. Serious infestations may be treated with insecticidal soap or with a chemical insecticide.
Leaves curl and turn yellow and flower buds and flowers become malformed. Leaves and stems are covered with a shiny, sticky substance on which a black, sooty mold may appear.	Aphids, ⅛-inch green, black, yellow, brown or pink insects that suck plant juices from the leaves, stems and buds. They secrete a sticky substance called honeydew on which black fungi grow.	Wash aphids off plants with warm, soapy water and then rinse. If this does not control the infestation, treat with insecticidal soap or a chemical insecticide.
Plants stop growing and leaves turn yellow and drop. When a plant is moved or disturbed, a cloud of tiny white insects appears.	Whiteflies, 1/16-inch insects that suck plant juices from the undersides of the leaves.	Wash infested plants with lukewarm, soapy water and then rinse. For severe infestations, treat with insecticidal soap or with a chemical insecticide.

PROBLEM	CAUSE	SOLUTION
Plant growth is stunted. Leaves become streaked in white or silver. Eventually, the leaves turn brown, curl and die. Flower buds may not open; if they do, the flowers will be distorted and streaked, spotted or edged in white, yellow or brown.	Thrips, $\frac{1}{16}$-inch, yellow, tan, brown or black insects that feed on buds, flowers and leaf joints. Thrips can hardly be seen on the plant. To confirm their presence, shake the plant over a piece of white paper; dark specks will fall onto the paper.	Remove and discard infested buds, flowers and leaves. Treat with an insecticide applied either to the plant or to the growing medium.
Small yellow or white spots appear on the upper leaf surfaces and tiny black spots appear on the undersides of the leaves. Leaves turn yellow and eventually dry out, turn brown and fall from the plant. Fine webbing appears between the leaves and around the flowers and flower buds.	Spider mites, pests that are nearly microscopic and that may be red, black, green or yellow.	Maintain high humidity to discourage spider mites, which thrive in hot, dry conditions. For a mild infestation, immerse the entire plant in mild soapy water; then rinse. For severe cases, treat with insecticidal soap or a miticide.
Plant growth slows or stops. Small flying insects are visible around plants.	Fungus gnats, black flies up to $\frac{1}{8}$ inch long. Adult flies carry diseases. The larvae hatch in the soil and feed on plant roots.	Use a household insect spray where insects are visible. Drench the growing medium with an insecticide, or dip the roots in an insecticidal solution and repot the plant in fresh medium and a clean pot.
Plants may not bloom; if they do, the flowers will be distorted, blotched or streaked, and flower stems may be twisted. Plant growth is stunted. Foliage becomes wrinkled, curls inward, has a dusty film on the undersides and may turn purple.	Cyclamen mite, a microscopic white, pale green or brown pest that feeds at the base of the plant and in leaves and buds. It is particularly troublesome when humidity is high.	Immerse lightly infested plants in 110° F water for 15 minutes, or treat them with a miticide. Discard heavily infested plants. Wash hands after handling infested plants in order not to carry insects to healthy plants.
White, yellow or light green serpentine trails appear on leaves, and eventually turn brown or black. Irregular blotches may also be present. The entire leaf eventually dries up and dies.	Leaf miners, $\frac{1}{10}$-inch fly larvae that tunnel between the layers of leaves and feed on the leaf tissue.	Remove infested foliage and apply a systemic insecticide to the growing medium.
Plant growth is stunted. Leaves become mottled, streaked or blotched with white, yellow, light green or brown. The edges of the leaves may roll up or become wrinkled. Flowers may be discolored, streaked, malformed or smaller than normal.	Viral infection.	Isolate diseased plants. In mild cases, symptoms may disappear by themselves. If the infection is severe, discard the plant and the growing medium and wash and rinse the pot in a 10 percent bleach solution before reusing it. There are no chemical controls.

PROBLEM	CAUSE	SOLUTION
Plant does not grow. Plant stems and crowns turn soft and brown at the soil line. Foliage at the base of the plant wilts, turns yellow and dies. Removing the plant from its pot reveals roots that are brown or black instead of white.	Root, stem and crown rot caused by fungi or bacteria that are especially active in wet growing medium.	Allow the soil to dry out between waterings. If the medium does not drain rapidly, repot the plant in new soilless medium and a shallower pot. Applying a fungicide to the growing medium may control the disease. Severely diseased plants should be discarded.
The stems of seedlings turn brown and the seedlings suddenly fall over and die.	Damping-off, a soilborne fungus disease.	Use only new, soilless sowing medium. Before sowing seeds, drench the medium with a fungicide. Be careful not to overwater seedlings.
The edges of leaves and petals appear scorched, or leaves fade and become dull and bleached, usually between the veins.	Excess light.	Move plants to an area that receives less light.
Flowers dry up. Leaves become limp or shrivel up, then turn dry and crisp, and fall from the plant.	Lack of water or low humidity.	If the entire plant displays symptoms, place it in a bucket of water; the water should be slightly higher than the rim of the pot so that the growing medium is submerged. Leave the plant in the water until it revives. Increase the frequency of watering, especially in summer. Increase the humidity around the plants with a humidifier or a pebble tray.
Leaves, especially at the base of the plant, turn yellow and become limp, and may fall from the plant. Flower buds may not form; if they do, they may rot before they open. Removing the plant from its pot reveals roots that are soft and brown or black instead of white; roots may have an unpleasant odor.	Growing medium is too wet.	Make sure that water does not stand in the saucer beneath the pot, and that the drainage holes are not clogged. Allow the growing medium to dry out between waterings. If the medium stays wet after infrequent watering, change to a more rapid-draining one.
Flowers fade and fall prematurely or do not form at all. Leaves lose their color without signs of disease. Lower leaves may drop. Plants do not grow, or they produce only spindly growth.	Insufficient light.	Move the plant into more direct sunlight or add supplemental fluorescent lights, especially during winter. Prune away any poor growth.

PROBLEM	CAUSE	SOLUTION
Foliage curls or becomes distorted, turns yellow and dies. A white powdery coating covers the leaves, stems and flower buds.	Powdery mildew, a fungus disease that is most serious when nights are cool and humidity is high.	In mild cases, mildew may be washed from leaves with warm, soapy water. In severe cases, treat with a fungicide. Be sure plants are not too close together and that air can circulate around them.
Leaves turn yellow, starting at the outer edges and working toward the middle, and then wilt, turn brown and die. The symptoms first appear at the bottom of the plant and then move upward. Growth stops and the plant dies.	Wilt diseases caused by bacteria or fungi.	Use new soilless potting medium. Drenching the growing medium with fungicide before planting may also help to prevent the disease. If the infection is severe, discard the plant and wash the pot and rinse it in a 10 percent bleach solution.
Hard, corky growths appear on the undersides of the leaves, and clusters of blisters appear on the upper surfaces. In severe cases, the blisters turn brown and the leaves turn yellow and drop.	Edema, the swelling of plant organs and tissues caused by waterlogged soil and poor light.	Remove all damaged leaves. Reduce the frequency of watering; if the medium does not drain quickly, repot the plant in fresh medium. Increase light intensity.
The undersides of leaves become covered with a powdery orange growth. Leaves may turn yellow and die, and the plant may fail to grow.	Rust, a fungus disease that is most prevalent in cool temperatures.	Raise the room temperature or move the plant to a warmer spot and remove infected leaves. Make sure that air can circulate around the plant, and be careful not to splash water on the leaves. Use a fungicide to prevent the disease from spreading.
Leaves develop gray or brown spots and eventually turn yellow and die. Flowers may not open; if they do, they are distorted or streaked. Flowers, flower buds, stems and leaves are covered with a gray or brown fuzzy growth.	Botrytis blight, also known as gray mold, a fungus disease. It appears most often in limited light, high humidity and cool temperatures.	Remove flowers as soon as they fade and discard any infected plant parts. In severe cases, treat with a fungicide. Space plants to ensure good air circulation. Be careful not to overwater or to splash water on the plants.
New leaves are small and pale and do not grow to normal size or develop normal color. Flowers do not form. Plant growth is irregular.	Lack of fertilizer.	Increase the frequency of fertilizing. Cut back the plant to restore its shape.
Red, brown or black spots appear on leaves and may be surrounded by yellow halos. As the spots increase in size and number and cover the leaves, the leaves die.	Leaf spot, which can be caused by bacteria or fungi.	Remove any infected leaves. When watering, do not wet the foliage. Space or thin plants to ensure that air circulates around them. In severe cases, treat with a fungicide.

69

TIPS AND TECHNIQUES

PLANTSCAPE: ARRANGING INDOOR PLANTS

Just as thoughtful design can make your outdoor garden more appealing to the eye, arranging your blossoming house-plants with an eye to color, shape and size can set them off to best advantage.

In a window with several shelves, organizing plants by color—that is, placing plants of the same color on the same shelf—will create horizontal lines of several different colors. And from across the room, especially, the effect can be striking. African violets work well in this type of design because they provide colorful blossoms throughout most of the year.

Vining plants such as allamanda, lipstick plant and wax vine, which make attractive displays in hanging pots, can also highlight the architectural details of your house. Placed on windowsills or mantels or even along the sides of an exposed staircase, falling blossoms create interest by drawing attention to the vertical, horizontal or diagonal lines of an interior.

POTASSIUM FROM BANANA PEEL

Bromeliads need potassium to encourage growth and to maintain a healthy appearance. One of the best sources of the mineral is banana peel. By cutting a small square of banana peel and placing it in the cup at the base of the plant (the space formed by the growth pattern of the leaves through which the plant receives most of its water and nutrients), you can give your bromeliad added vigor and color.

SELECTING FLOWERING PLANTS

Appearance says a lot about a plant, but to buy one that is really healthy, you must check more than its appearance—the fullness of the plant, its color and the evenness of its leaves. Check around the stem and under the leaves for signs of insects or disease that may not be visible at arm's length. Then check the drain hole. If you see roots growing out of the hole, the plant is pot-bound; choose another. A plant that is in full bloom might not continue to flower when you get it home; you will have a better chance at prolonged blooming if you choose a plant that has more buds than blossoms.

Once you bring the plant indoors, give it a good watering, and isolate it for at least a week to make sure that it is insect-free, so it doesn't spread insects to your other plants.

COOLER TEMPERATURES FOR BETTER BLOSSOMS

Flowering plants generally require more light and cooler temperatures than foliage plants. Fuchsia and gardenias prefer constantly cooler temperatures, and cyclamen and Christmas cactus plants may not blossom at all if they are kept in a warm room. For more and longer-lasting flowers, place such plants in the cooler corners of the house, away from heat vents, radiators and appliances, such as refrigerators and television sets, that give off heat.

FRAGRANT BLOSSOMS INDOORS

Growing blossoming houseplants for their aroma can be as rewarding as growing them for their colorful flowers. Among the best-known aromatic plants are the jasmines, many of which will grow in the house. Citrus blossoms, too, have a pervasive scent, and gardenias, though difficult to grow indoors, also provide an attractive perfume. Others that do well indoors are trachelospermum, stephanotis and heliotrope.

If you want to have several types of fragrant plants, be sure to place them in separate parts of the house so that the scents will not compete with one another; the aromas of jasmine and citrus, especially, can travel some distance from the plant. Or, choose plants that blossom at different times of the year, to give your house different fragrances during different seasons.

CONTROLLING INSECTS WITHOUT INSECTICIDES

Aphids can be as troublesome for flowering houseplants as they are for outdoor plants. And chemical insecticides are best avoided indoors. A safe alternative is to use a tea made with tobacco (from a crushed cigarette, for example) soaked in water. Sprayed on plants, the tea will help to control aphids, without spotting the leaves.

Whiteflies will succumb to a different treatment: a household vacuum cleaner. With the dusting brush attachment, you can remove these insects from both the plant and the air around the plant. At first, you may have to vacuum your plants several times a week, but once you have removed the eggs and hatching larvae, it will be hard for the pests to reestablish themselves. Don't forget to vacuum the undersides of the leaves, where spider mites live.

ENCOURAGING BROMELIADS TO BLOSSOM

A ripening apple can induce bromeliads to blossom. If you have an urn plant, guzmania or flaming-sword that resists blossoming, enclose it in a plastic bag with the apple for a week; within six weeks, you should see the result. The blossom is brought on by the plant's exposure to ethylene, a gas that apples give off as they ripen.

SPENDING THE SUMMER OUTDOORS

Except for gesneriads, whose leaves spot from cold water, most houseplants benefit from spending time outdoors during summer. Blossoming plants especially appreciate outdoor light, which is much more intense than the light they receive in your sunniest window. But when you take them outside, place them in shade or partial shade at first, and then gradually move them to a sunnier location, so as not to shock them.

Even when your plants are outdoors, make sure they receive enough water. Being exposed to wind will dry them out quickly, so a sheltered site is best.

Wait to take your plants outdoors until all chance of frost has passed, and be sure to bring them back indoors before cold weather arrives. When you return the plants to the house in the fall, check for signs of insects; examine leaves and blossoms and carefully remove each plant from its pot to look for pests that may have entered through the drainage holes.

6

DICTIONARY OF FLOWERING HOUSEPLANTS

Simply put, flowering houseplants are those blossoming plants that can be grown successfully indoors. This group naturally includes a large number of tropical plants, which, when brought to the temperate zones, require the constant warmth of an indoor environment. Still others, like the spring-flowering bulbs, begonias and chrysanthemums that are found in the garden during much of the year, can be brought into the house to provide color during the colder seasons. And some, like pepper plants and coffee and orange trees, which are normally grown for their fruit, bring equal rewards when grown for their blossoms.

The Dictionary of Flowering Houseplants contains more than 100 genera that are the most amenable to indoor growing. Each entry consists of a general description of the genus, along with descriptions of a number of distinct species, to help you distinguish plants that may be grown for fragrance, those that are suitable for hanging baskets and those that bloom at particular times of year.

Whether flowering houseplants are grown for their color, for the unusual shape of their blooms or for fragrance, their blossoms remain the center of attention. For each entry in the dictionary, a separate section entitled "Growing Conditions" will help you to achieve healthy plants and, above all, abundant, long-lasting blossoms. The needs of individual plants with regard to growing medium, water and light are described, as are the best means of propagation. Where appropriate, instructions for forcing plants to bloom out of season are included.

ABUTILON PICTUM

ACALYPHA HISPIDA

Abutilon (a-BEW-ti-lon)
Flowering maple

Shrubby, 3-foot plant that usually has lobed, 2- to 3-inch leaves. The flowers are drooping, funnel- or bell-shaped, 2 inches long, and white, yellow, orange or reddish purple. They are paperlike in consistency and hang from the leaf axils. Flowering maple blooms year round.

Selected species and varieties. *A. hybridum,* Chinese lantern, has white, red, yellow or orange flowers, and light green or variegated leaves. *A. megapotamicum,* trailing abutilon, has arrow-shaped leaves that are sometimes lobed. The flowers are two-toned, red and yellow. The branches are slender and flexible, making this a good plant for a hanging basket. 'Variegata' has mottled leaves. *A. pictum* has lobed leaves and flowers of yellow or yellow-orange, with deep red veins. 'Pleniflorum' has double flowers. 'Thompsonii' has variegated leaves.

Growing conditions. Grow flowering maple in direct light in a warm room that has medium humidity. Keep the growing medium evenly moist from spring through fall; in winter, allow the medium to dry out between waterings. Cut the stems back in the spring before new growth starts, and pinch out growing tips to keep the plants compact. Fertilize every two weeks when the plant is in growth or in flower. Repot in the spring when necessary. Propagate flowering maple from stem cuttings or from seeds. Flowering maple may be damaged by mealybugs, spider mites, scales, whiteflies, root knot nematodes, leaf spot and virus.

―

Acalypha (ak-a-LEE-fa)
Copperleaf

Bushy plant noted for its long, slender, drooping, fuzzy plumes of flowers that bloom most abundantly in fall and winter. Foliage is coarse, usually toothed and prominently veined. Plants are 2 to 3 feet tall when mature.

Selected species and varieties. *A. hispida,* chenille plant, has broad, oval, hairy leaves and hanging spikes of red or purple flowers. 'Alba' has white flowers with a light pink cast.

Growing conditions. Chenille plant will grow well in either direct light or bright light, and in average to warm temperature. It grows best when humidity is high. Keep the growing medium evenly moist and fertilize every month. To keep plants bushy, cut them back in early spring before new growth starts. Propagate chenille plant from stem cuttings. Chenille plant is susceptible to leaf spot, root rot, powdery mildew, mealybugs and scales.

―

Achimenes (a-KIM-e-neez)
Magic flower

Bushy plant having stems that may be erect or trailing and flowers that are tubular, five-lobed and slightly shimmering. Species having trailing stems are suitable for hanging baskets.

Selected species and varieties. *A. longiflora,* widow's tears, has 12-inch trailing stems. The foliage is oval to lance-shaped, 3½ inches long, shiny, sometimes hairy, and toothed. The flowers are satiny, 1 to 2½ inches wide, and blue, white, pink, yellow, red or purple. The plants bloom primarily during the summer. 'Alba' has white flowers with a yellow eye and a dark purple line on each petal. 'Ambroise Verschaffelt' is similar to 'Alba', but with heavier purple markings and purple dots in the throat. 'Galatea' has lavender petals with a white and purple throat. 'Major' has large, 3-inch flowers of light violet with a dark purple throat. 'Margarita' has pure white petals and a yellow throat. 'Paul Arnold' has deep purple flowers; the throat is white and yellow and dotted in red.

Growing conditions. Grow magic flower in bright light or under fluorescent lights. The room should be warm and have average humidity. Keep the potting medium evenly moist, being careful not to splash the leaves with water, which may cause spotting. Fertilize monthly when the plant is in growth or in flower. After the plant has flowered, withhold water until the foliage wilts and dies. Store the rhizomes at 45° F over the winter, placing them in a plastic bag filled with dry peat moss, vermiculite or perlite. In spring, divide the rhizomes and repot. Magic flower can also be propagated by stem cuttings or from seeds. It is vulnerable to attack by aphids, mealybugs, thrips and crown rot.

ACHIMENES LONGIFLORA

Aechmea (EEK-mee-a)
Air pine, living-vase, urn plant

A bromeliad having long, stiff leaves that grow in a rosette at the base of the plant and form a cuplike space that can hold water. The flowers are very showy and appear in spikes. Plants grow up to 2 feet tall indoors.

Selected species and varieties. *A. chantinii* has olive green to brown leaves that bear distinct pinkish gray bands. The flowers are red tipped in yellow. *A. fasciata* has leaves that are toothed and are streaked or banded with silver or white. The flower spikes grow up to 2 feet long; tiny blue or purple flowers appear amid pink to red bracts. 'Albo Marginata' has white margins on the inside of the leaves. 'Variegata' has green and white striped leaves. *A. fulgens,* coralberry, has stiff green leaves covered with gray dust; the flower spikes have oblong red berries tipped with blue or purple flowers.

Growing conditions. Grow urn plant in bright light in a warm room with medium humidity. The growing medium should be coarse, with extra bark or osmunda fiber added; keep it evenly moist but not wet. Water should be kept in the cup at the base of the plant. Fertilize monthly with quarter-strength liquid fertilizer solution. There are commercial preparations available that induce flowering in bromeliads. Propagate by removing and planting the side shoots that grow at the base of the plant after it flowers, by division or from seed. Bromeliads are usually not bothered by insects or diseases, but occasionally scales or crown rot may attack.

AECHMEA FASCIATA

AESCHYNANTHUS PULCHER

AGAPANTHUS ORIENTALIS

Aeschynanthus (ess-kuh-NAN-thus)
Basket plant

Graceful vining plant with thin, 2- to 3-foot stems, leathery leaves and drooping, tubular, five-lobed flowers at the ends of the stems. The flower buds are long and slender, resemble tubes of lipstick and bloom in spring.

Selected species and varieties. *A. pulcher,* scarlet basket vine, has small, oval, waxy, light green leaves and clusters of showy red, 2-inch flowers that have yellow throats. The outer petals, called calyces, are leaf-shaped and green. *A. radicans,* formerly designated *A. parviflorus,* lipstick plant, has deep, glossy green, 2-inch, lance-shaped, toothed leaves and 1- to 2-inch red flowers tipped in yellow. The calyces are deep purple.

Growing conditions. Lipstick plant prefers direct light in winter and bright light the rest of the year, warm temperatures and high humidity. The growing medium should be very rich and evenly moist at all times. Fertilize monthly during spring and summer. After the plant flowers, cut the stems back to 6 inches to encourage new growth. Propagate by stem cuttings taken in spring. Basket plant can attract aphids, mealybugs and spider mites and may develop root rot.

▬

African lily see *Agapanthus*
African violet see *Saintpaulia*

▬

Agapanthus (ag-a-PAN-thus)

Stout, rhizomatous plant that has strap-shaped leaves, erect stems and large, round clusters of tubular to bell-shaped flowers that bloom primarily during the summer.

Selected species and varieties. *A. africanus,* African lily, lily-of-the-Nile, grows 18 to 24 inches tall and has linear, rich green leaves 1 inch wide. The flowers are funnel-shaped, 1½ inches long and deep blue-violet, blooming in clusters of up to 30 flowers. 'Peter Pan' grows 12 to 18 inches tall and has deep blue flowers. *A. orientalis* grows 24 inches tall and has strap-shaped leaves 2 inches wide. Flowers are funnel-shaped, 2 inches long and blue, blooming in clusters of up to 100 flowers. 'Albidus' has white flowers. 'Mooreanus' has dark blue flowers and narrow leaves. 'Nanus' is dwarf and compact. 'Variegatus' has striped foliage. Headbourne hybrids are 30 inches tall and have flowers in various shades of blue.

Growing conditions. Place tubs of agapanthus in a room with average temperature, direct light and medium humidity. In summer, protect from direct midday sun. Keep the growing medium evenly moist in spring, summer and fall, and allow it to dry out between waterings during the winter. Fertilize every two weeks during spring and summer. Agapanthus grows best if it is pot-bound, and, in summer, benefits from being moved outdoors to a sheltered spot. Propagate by division or from seeds. Agapanthus can be damaged by virus, mealybugs, scales and thrips.

Air pine see *Aechmea*

—

Allamanda (al-a-MAN-da)

Vining plant that grows from 2 to 6 feet tall and has large, fragrant, funnel-shaped yellow or purple flowers in spring and summer.

Selected species and varieties. *A. cathartica,* golden trumpet, is a vigorous plant with whorled, waxy, dark green leaves and 5-inch, bright yellow flowers. 'Grandiflora' is dwarf and compact, with lemon yellow flowers. 'Hendersonii' has leathery leaves and large flowers with buds tinged in brown. 'Nobilis' has bright, clear yellow flowers that have a sweet fragrance. 'Schottii' flowers have a dark stripe on the throat. 'Stansill's Double' is a double-flowered variety. 'Williamsii' has yellow flowers with reddish brown throats.

Growing conditions. Grow allamanda in a warm room with direct light and high humidity. Allow the growing medium to become dry between waterings in fall and winter; keep the medium evenly moist during spring and summer. Feed every two weeks when the plants are in growth or in flower. Cut plants back in early spring before new growth starts. Large plants can be trained to cover a wall; smaller plants should be given a small trellis or support on which to grow. Propagate by stem cuttings taken in spring or summer. Allamanda can be attacked by mealybugs, scales and whiteflies.

—

Amaryllis see *Hippeastrum*
Amazon lily see *Eucharis*

—

Ananas (a-NAN-us)
Pineapple

A bromeliad having long, stiff, slender, spiny leaves that grow in a rosette at the base of the plant and form a cuplike cavity that can hold water. Flowers form on thick, sturdy stems and are followed by cylindrical, edible fruits. A tuft of foliage grows at the top of the fruit.

Selected species and varieties. *A. bracteatus,* red pineapple, has 2- to 3-foot leaves and showy red flowers with long, spiny bracts. Fruits can grow up to 1 foot long. *A. comosus,* common pineapple, has 2- to 3-foot leaves and violet or reddish flowers. Fruits can grow up to 1 foot long. 'Porteanus' has leaves with a central yellow stripe. 'Variegatus' has leaves with ivory and pink stripes on the margins. *A. nanus,* a dwarf variety that is most suitable for indoor growing, produces a fruit about 1½ to 2 inches long. Leaves grow 12 to 15 inches long; flowers are purple.

Growing conditions. Grow pineapple in a room with average to high temperature, direct light and high humidity. The growing medium should be loose and well drained, with additional coarse perlite, bark chips or osmunda fiber added. Keep the medium evenly moist, and keep the cup at the base of the plant filled with water. Fertilize monthly with

ALLAMANDA CATHARTICA

ANANAS COMOSUS

ANTHURIUM SCHERZERANUM

APHELANDRA SQUARROSA

quarter-strength liquid fertilizer. Propagate either by cutting off the top of the fruit with the foliage intact and planting the entire top after it has dried for several days, or by removing the offshoots that form at the base of the plant. Pineapples are generally free of insects and diseases, but may attract scales or develop crown rot.

Anthurium (an-THUR-ee-um)
Tailflower

Tropical plant suitable for growing indoors. Leaves are thick and firm, and have prominent veins. The flowers are tiny and found along a tail-like structure called a spadix; they are surrounded by colorful, shiny, 4- to 12-inch bracts called spathes. Flowers may appear all year and each flower will last for a month or more.

Selected species and varieties. *A. andreanum,* flamingo lily, has long, narrow, oval to heart-shaped leaves. The spathe is heart-shaped, 4 to 6 inches long, puckered, highly polished and salmon-red; the spadix is golden yellow, often with a white band. Plants grow 2 to 3 feet tall. *A. × cultorum* is a group of complex hybrids similar in appearance to flamingo lily. 'Atrosanguineum' has dark red spathes. 'Giganteum' has large, salmon-red spathes. 'Reidii' has very large, deep pink spathes. 'Rhodochlorum' has very large spathes that are up to 12 inches long and rose-colored. *A. × roseum* has flat spathes of white to rose and white to pink spadices. 'Album' has creamy white spathes; 'Roseum' has a spathe that is soft rose on the upper surface and white to rose on the underside; 'Salmoneum' has a yellow-salmon spathe. *A. scherzeranum,* flamingo flower, has very narrow, lance-shaped leaves on 1- to 2-foot plants. The spathe is shiny and scarlet; the spadix is orange-red or golden yellow and is often twisted. 'Atrosanguineum' has dark red spathes. 'Rothschildianum' has a red spathe specked in white and a yellow spadix.

Growing conditions. Tailflower should be grown where light is limited, air is warm and humidity is high. If the humidity is too low, the plant will not flower. The growing medium should be rich, fast-draining and constantly wet when the plants are in flower. At others times, keep the medium evenly moist. If aerial roots develop, cover them with moist sphagnum peat moss. Fertilize monthly. Propagate by removing the offshoots at the base of the plant, by division, by stem cuttings or from seed. Insects do not cause problems; leaf spot may develop.

Aphelandra (af-e-LAN-dra)

Tropical plant having large leaves that are topped by 4- to 8-inch spikes of tubular flowers.

Selected species and varieties. *A. squarrosa,* zebra plant, has oval, 6-inch leaves that are glossy green with prominent white to silver veins. Pale to golden yellow flowers with orange bracts appear off and on throughout the year. Indoors, plants grow about 12 to 18 inches high.

Growing conditions. Zebra plant is easy to grow indoors in an average or warm room with average humidity and bright light. The growing medium should be evenly moist from spring through fall; in winter allow it to dry out slightly between waterings. Fertilize every two weeks from spring through early fall. In early spring, plants may be cut back to encourage compact growth. Propagate by stem cuttings taken in spring or from seed. Zebra plant can attract mealybugs.

Ardisia (ar-DIZ-ee-a)

Genus of tropical and semitropical trees and shrubs, one species of which is grown indoors. Leaves are leathery; flowers are small, white or rose, and bloom in clusters.

Selected species and varieties. *A. crenata,* coralberry, has lance-shaped leaves on plants that grow to 3 feet tall indoors. After plants reach 18 to 24 inches in height, they lose their lower leaves and look like small trees if they are not cut back each year. The flowers are ¼ inch long, white or pink, and fragrant. They bloom on new growth that starts in midwinter to early spring, and are followed by long-lasting, bright red, ¼-inch berries that appear during the winter holiday season. 'Alba' has white flowers and berries.

Growing conditions. Coralberry prefers a room with average temperature and humidity, and should be placed in bright light. Use an all-purpose potting medium and keep it evenly moist from summer through winter. In late winter, cut plants back to encourage compactness, new growth and flowering. Until new growth appears, allow the medium to dry out between waterings. Fertilize every two weeks from spring through fall. Propagate by stem cuttings, by air layering or from seed. Coralberry is susceptible to scales and leaf spot.

Atamasco lily see *Zephyranthes*
Azalea see *Rhododendron*
Basket plant see *Aeschynanthus*

Begonia (be-GO-nee-a)

Very large genus of plants having thousands of species and varieties that can be grown as houseplants. Some species are fibrous- or tuberous-rooted and have loose clusters of small flowers. Other species are rhizomatous and, although they flower, are grown for their brightly colored and marked foliage. Flowers are single or double, and, depending on the species, white, pink, red, orange or yellow.

Selected species and varieties. *B. coccinea,* angel-wing begonia, is fibrous-rooted. It can grow to 3 feet tall and has thick, toothed, heart-shaped leaves. The foliage is green with a wavy red margin on the upper surface, and a red underside. Flowers are waxy and coral-red, and bloom in spring. *B. × hiemalis,* Rieger begonia, is a group of hybrids with large, single or double, white, pink, red, orange or yellow flowers that bloom in winter and spring. Plants grow 6 to 12 inches tall. *B. × rex-cultorum,*

ARDISIA CRENATA

BEGONIA × SEMPERFLORENS-CULTORUM

BEGONIA × TUBERHYBRIDA

BILLBERGIA VITTATA

rex begonia, is a group of hybrids of *B. rex*. Most are rhizomatous, and all are known for the highly colored leaves, which are marbled, blotched or marked with green, purple, red, pink, bronze, gray, black or silver. The leaves are shaped like an elephant's ear and may be smooth or textured. Flowers are white or pink, but are not showy; they bloom in spring. Plants grow about 12 inches tall. *B. × semperflorens-cultorum,* wax begonia, has small, round, shiny, green, variegated or reddish bronze leaves, and 1-inch flowers of white, pink or red. It is fibrous-rooted, grows 6 to 8 inches high and blooms all year. *B. × tuberhybrida,* tuberous begonia, has single or double, 2- to 4-inch flowers that bloom in spring and summer over heart-shaped leaves. They come in all colors, and some resemble roses or camellias. The plants grow 6 to 12 inches high and some varieties can be grown in hanging baskets. 'Nonstop' is a very free flowering variety with semidouble flowers on 8- to 10-inch plants.

Growing conditions. Most begonias grow best in bright light; rex begonias prefer limited light. All begonias prefer average to warm temperatures. All except tuberous and rex begonias grow well in average humidity; tuberous and rex begonias like high humidity. Grow all begonias in rich potting medium and keep the medium evenly moist except in winter, when it should be allowed to dry out slightly between waterings. All begonias like monthly fertilizing when they are in growth or in flower. Wax begonias like to be pot-bound and can be pinched to keep them compact. Propagate angel-wing from stem cuttings, rex begonias by dividing the rhizomes or from leaf cuttings, tuberous begonias by dividing the tubers or from stem cuttings, wax begonias from seed or stem cuttings. Begonias are vulnerable to attack by whiteflies, aphids, mealybugs, spider and cyclamen mites, powdery mildew, botrytis blight and leaf spot. Seedlings can be damaged by damping-off.

—

Bellflower see *Campanula*

—

Billbergia (bil-BER-jee-a)
Vase plant

A bromeliad having stiff, tall, slender leaves that form rosettes that can hold water at the base of the plant. Tubular flowers bloom in spikes in spring; they have green, red or blue petals and showy bracts of many colors.

Selected species and varieties. *B. amoena* has narrow, gray-green, 2-foot leaves with silver cross-bands; flowers have pale green petals edged in blue, rose bracts and bloom in arching spikes. *B. nutans,* friendship plant, queen's tears, has an open rosette of toothed, 1½-foot, arching, silvery bronze to green leaves. The flowers nod and have green petals edged in blue or lavender, pink sepals and bright rose bracts. *B. pyramidalis,* foolproof plant, has 3-foot, toothed, dark green leaves banded with light gray. The flowers are cone-shaped, with red petals edged in violet and bright orange-red bracts. *B. vittata* has 3-foot, leathery, olive to purplish green, silver-banded leaves with red spines. The petals are blue, the bracts red. There are many hybrids of vase plant, many having brightly colored or spotted foliage.

Growing conditions. Grow vase plant in a warm room with average humidity and direct light. The growing medium should be extra rich and well drained, and should dry out between waterings. Keep water in the cup at the base of the plant. Fertilize monthly during spring and summer with quarter-strength liquid fertilizer. Propagate by removing the offshoots that form at the base of the plant. Vase plant can be damaged by scales.

—

Bird-of-paradise see *Strelitzia*

Black-eyed Susan vine see *Thunbergia*

Blood lily see *Haemanthus*

Blushing bromeliad see *Nidularium*

—

Bougainvillea (boo-gan-VIL-ee-a)

Woody, spiny, tropical vine that can be grown indoors for its showy, papery, 1-inch bracts of white, yellow, copper, pink, red or purple that surround tiny flowers. Indoors, bougainvillea blooms in spring and summer, and can grow up to 6 feet high.

Selected species and varieties. *B.* × *buttiana* has oval leaves and crisp bracts of crimson to orange that fade to purple or mauve as they age. 'Barbara Karst' has bright red flowers and tends to be bushy in its growth habit. 'Praetoria' has golden bronze bracts suffused with pink and yellow. 'Temple Fire' is bushy in habit and has brick red bracts.

Growing conditions. Bougainvillea needs direct light and average to high humidity. It should be cool and dry during the winter so it will go dormant. Grow in all-purpose growing medium. Fertilize monthly from early spring through late summer. To be grown as a vine, it needs to be tied to a support. After it flowers, it can be cut back and forced to grow into a bushy shape, but such pruning inhibits future flowering. Propagate from stem cuttings taken in late spring or from seed. Bougainvillea is generally not susceptible to insect or disease damage, but you may occasionally see mealybugs.

—

Brazilian plume flower see *Justicia*

—

Browallia (bro-WAL-ee-a)

Upright or trailing plant that has bell-shaped, velvety, 2-inch, purple, blue or white flowers that may appear all year, but bloom most abundantly in summer and fall. Trailing varieties grow well in hanging baskets.

Selected species and varieties. *B. speciosa* has masses of satiny flowers, and oval leaves. The Bells varieties have stems that trail 10 to 12 inches from the center of the plant, and white, light blue, dark blue or purple flowers. The Trolls varieties are more compact, with 8- to 10-inch stems and flowers of blue or white.

BOUGAINVILLEA × BUTTIANA

BROWALLIA SPECIOSA

BRUNFELSIA PAUCIFLORA 'MACRANTHA'

CALCEOLARIA CRENATIFLORA

Growing conditions. In winter, grow browallia in direct light; during the rest of the year, give it bright light. Temperature can be average or warm, humidity average. Plant in a rich growing medium and keep it evenly moist. Fertilize every two weeks from spring through fall, and monthly in winter. Pinch out growing tips if you want a compact plant. After the plant has flowered, it often declines, and should be discarded. New plants can be propagated from seed or from cuttings. Browallia sometimes attracts aphids and can be damaged by virus and wilt diseases.

—

Brunfelsia (brun-FEL-see-a)

Genus of tropical shrubs and small trees, some of which can be grown indoors. The flowers, which are often fragrant, are tubular or bell-shaped and bloom in loose clusters. Blooms are white or blue when they open, and often change color quickly as they age. Flowers appear most abundantly in summer and fall, but may bloom off and on all year.

Selected species and varieties. B. *australis,* yesterday-today-and-tomorrow, has broad leaves and 1½-inch flowers that are deep blue the first day, lighter colored the second day and white the third day. B. *pauciflora,* formerly known as B. *calycina,* has larger flower clusters and oblong, shiny leaves. The flowers are 1½ to 2 inches across and purple to deep blue, with wavy margins. 'Eximia' is also known as yesterday-today-and-tomorrow because the 2-inch flowers change in color from deep blue to light blue, to white. 'Floribunda' is a dwarf form whose abundant flowers also change color; 'Macrantha' has very large flowers.

Growing conditions. Brunfelsia needs cool temperatures in winter, and will grow in cool or average temperatures in spring through fall. Humidity should be average; light should be bright. Pot in an extra-rich growing medium and keep it evenly moist. When the plant stops blooming, usually in late spring, reduce water and cut the plant back if necessary to keep it compact. The prunings can be used to root new plants. Fertilize every other week when plants are in growth or in flower. They bloom best when pot-bound. Brunfelsia is susceptible to scales.

—

Buttonhole orchid see *Epidendrum*
Busy Lizzie see *Impatiens*

—

Calceolaria (kal-see-o-LAR-ee-a)

Broad genus, one species of which is an annual that is widely grown as a houseplant. Plants have masses of red, yellow, orange or brown blooms with unique "pockets," or pouches, at the front of the flowers.

Selected species and varieties. C. *crenatiflora,* pocketbook plant, has clusters of 1- to 3-inch flowers that may be either solid-colored or spotted. Plants vary in height, depending on the variety, from 6 to 15 inches. The foliage is oval, toothed and up to 8 inches long at the bottom of the plant, decreasing in size on the upper portions of the stems. 'Anytime' is an early-blooming, compact variety growing 6 to 8 inches tall with 2-inch flowers. 'Bright 'n Early' stands 7 to 9 inches high and has clusters of 1-inch flowers. 'Glorious' grows 8 to 10 inches tall and has 2½- to 3-inch flowers.

Growing conditions. Pocketbook plant needs a cool room with average humidity and indirect light. Grow in rich potting medium, and allow the medium to dry out between waterings. When watering, do not allow water to touch the leaves or the leaves may rot. Fertilize once a month when the plants are growing, and stop fertilizing when the flower buds have set. Pocketbook plant is grown from seed; sow seed in late spring to early fall for blooming the following winter and spring. If you grow your own plants from seed, be sure to maintain night temperature below 50° F or flower buds will not form. After the plants have bloomed, they will decline and should be discarded. Seedlings are susceptible to damping-off; when transplanting them, do not plant them too deep or stem rot will occur. Insects that may bother pocketbook plant are thrips, aphids and whiteflies.

CALENDULA OFFICINALIS

Calendula (ka-LEN-du-la)

Annual that can be grown indoors for its brightly colored, daisylike flowers.

Selected species and varieties. *C. officinalis,* pot marigold, has 2½- to 3-inch flowers with crisp petals of orange, yellow, gold or apricot. Blooms are single or double and bloom atop fuzzy, 10- to 20-inch stems. 'Bon Bon' is the most compact variety, growing 10 inches tall. 'Coronet' grows 12 inches high. 'Fiesta Gitana', sometimes designated as 'Gypsy Festival', is also 12 inches high. Plants can be grown to bloom at any time of year.

Growing conditions. Pot marigold must be grown in a cool room with average humidity. It should be potted in all-purpose growing medium that is kept evenly moist, and placed in direct light. Fertilize monthly during its growing and flowering period. Although pot marigold can be grown from stem cuttings, it is usually propagated from seed. Keeping flowers picked as soon as they fade will prolong its life, but since it is an annual, it will die after it flowers and must be discarded. Pot marigold attracts aphids, mealybugs, scales, thrips and whiteflies, and may be prone to botrytis blight, leaf spot, powdery mildew, and root and stem rot.

CAMELLIA JAPONICA

Calla lily see *Zantedeschia*

Camellia (ka-MEEL-ee-a)

Evergreen shrub that can be grown indoors for its single or double, waxy flowers of white, pink or red. The flowers of some varieties are two-toned. Plants grow 1 to 4 feet tall, depending on their age and how they are pruned, and have glossy, leathery, dark green leaves.

CAMPANULA ISOPHYLLA

Selected species and varieties. *C. japonica,* Japanese camellia, is a dense plant that has thick, oval, pointed, 3- to 4-inch leaves. The flowers are 3 to 5 inches across and bloom in winter and spring. *C. reticulata,* net-vein camellia, has 4-inch leaves with prominent veins. Flowers are up to 6 inches across, have wavy petals, and appear in winter and spring. *C. sasanqua,* Sasanqua camellia, is a loose plant with slender 2-inch leaves. Flowers are 2 to 3 inches across and bloom in fall and winter.

Growing conditions. Grow camellias where temperatures are cool, humidity is average to high and light is bright. When plants are in bloom, a cool temperature and high humidity will prolong the life of the flowers and prevent bud drop. Potting medium must be extra rich, well drained and kept constantly moist. Fertilize with a plant food for acid-loving plants in early spring, late spring and midsummer. To produce larger flowers, remove all but one flower bud in a cluster. After the plant has flowered, cut it back to encourage compactness, and use the prunings to propagate new plants. Camellia will benefit from being placed outdoors in summer in light shade. Scales, aphids, mealybugs, root knot nematodes and spider mites are the insects that most commonly attack camellia. The plant is also susceptible to a disease called camellia petal blight.

—

Campanula (kam-PAN-u-la)
Bellflower

Genus of annuals, biennials and perennials, one species of which is commonly grown indoors. The flowers are bell-shaped, 2 inches across, bloom in spikes or clusters, and are white, blue, lavender or pink.

Selected species and varieties. *C. isophylla,* Italian bellflower, is a trailing plant suitable for a hanging basket. Leaves at the base of the plant are heart-shaped and toothed, and those farther along the stem are lance-shaped. Flowers are blue-violet, 1½ inches across and bloom in clusters. 'Alba', star-of-Bethlehem, is a dainty plant with thin stems, oval leaves and white, star-shaped flowers. 'Mayii' has coarser leaves with white hairs, and large, pale blue flowers. All bloom in summer through late fall.

Growing conditions. Grow Italian bellflower in a cool room with average or high humidity and direct light. The growing medium should be rich, well drained and evenly moist. Fertilize monthly in spring through fall, and pinch out growing tips if plants become leggy. Plants are grown from seed sown in late fall to flower early the following summer; they are light-sensitive and will not bloom, unless artificially lighted, in the short days of winter and spring. Plants may also be propagated by stem cuttings in spring. They are best treated as annuals, since they do not perform well after they bloom. Italian bellflower is subject to attack by aphids, botrytis blight, leaf spot, powdery mildew, and root and stem rot.

—

Cape jasmine see *Gardenia*
Cape leadwort see *Plumbago*

Cape primrose see *Streptocarpus*

Capsicum (KAP-si-kum)
Pepper

Plant that has small white flowers that are followed by green, red, yellow or purple edible fruit. One species is grown as a decorative houseplant.

Selected species and varieties. *C. annuum*, ornamental pepper, has tiny, star-shaped flowers that bloom in early summer, but the plant is grown for its masses of small fruits, which form during the summer and fall and are more colorful than the flowers. Fruits, which are edible but usually very hot, are round, tapered or cone-shaped, and change in color from white to ivory, chartreuse, purple, red or orange as they mature. Depending on the variety, plants grow 4 to 12 inches high. 'Fireworks' has cone-shaped fruit on a spreading, 6- to 8-inch plant, and is suitable for growing in a hanging basket. 'Holiday Flame' has slim fruit on a 12-inch plant. 'Holiday Time' grows only 4 to 6 inches high and has cone-shaped fruit that develops in a central crown along the main stem. 'Red Missile' has large, tapered fruit on a 10-inch plant.

Growing conditions. Grow ornamental pepper in direct light, warm temperature and average to high humidity. It grows well in all-purpose potting medium as long as it is kept evenly moist. To keep plants compact, pinch out growing tips; to ensure that fruit will set, tap the branches gently when they are in flower to aid pollination. Pick the peppers frequently to keep the plant producing. Ornamental pepper is an annual and will die after it has finished flowering and fruiting, when it must be discarded. New plants can be grown from seed. Seed can be sown in spring to produce fruiting plants in summer and fall; seed sown in summer will produce plants that bear fruits for the winter holidays. Ornamental pepper is vulnerable to attack by aphids, virus and damping-off.

Carissa (ka-RIS-a)

Genus of tropical evergreen trees and shrubs, one species of which is grown as a houseplant. Plants are spiny; leaves are leathery. White or pinkish fragrant flowers bloom in clusters and are followed by showy, leathery berries. Carissa oozes a milky sap when a leaf is broken or a stem is cut.

Selected species and varieties. *C. grandiflora*, Natal plum, has dark green, shiny, oval, 1-inch leaves and long, forked spines. The flowers, which have long tubes ending in five flat lobes, are fragrant, waxy white and appear in small clusters at any time of year; each flower is 1½ to 2 inches across. The fruits are plumlike in appearance and are edible, but are tart and taste more like cranberries. Plants may grow to 3 feet tall; smaller varieties that grow about 12 to 18 inches high are available. 'Horizontalis', 'Prostrata' and 'Tuttlei' are compact, spreading varieties. 'Minima' is a dwarf form. 'Nana Compacta' is a low-growing variety without thorns.

Growing conditions. Natal plum likes to be grown where temperature and humidity are average and light is direct. Keep the growing medium moist, and fertilize every three to four months. Prune out growing tips to keep the plant compact. Natal plum

CAPSICUM ANNUUM

CARISSA GRANDIFLORA

CATTLEYA HYBRID

CATTLEYA HYBRID

can be increased either by stem cuttings taken at any time or from seed. Natal plum can be damaged by spider mites, scales and thrips.

—

Carpet plant see *Episcia*

—

Cattleya (KAT-lee-a)

Orchid that has thick, leathery foliage and fragrant flowers that appear in sprays. The blooms have three narrow petals, two broader petals and a large, tubular lip at the bottom front of the flower.

Selected species and varieties. There are a large number of *Cattleya* species and hybrids that have 5- to 7-inch flowers of white, yellow, pink, blue, green, red, lavender or purple. Plants grow 12 to 18 inches high and, depending on the species and variety, bloom at different times of year.

Growing conditions. To grow cattleyas in the house is a challenge even for the experts. If light intensity is too high, the normally yellow-green leaves will turn more yellow and burn; if the plant receives insufficient light, it may not flower. Provide plants with direct light, a warm room and high humidity. Use a growing medium made for orchids, one containing extra fir or redwood bark or osmunda fiber. Fertilize monthly from midfall to midspring, and twice monthly at other times of year, using a complete fertilizer. When plants are in bud or in bloom, they like to be kept evenly moist; at other times, allow the medium to dry slightly between waterings. Stems are long and need to be staked. Cattleyas benefit from being placed in a greenhouse when not in bloom, or outdoors in summer and early fall. When dividing the rhizomes for propagation, make sure that each division contains three to six pseudobulbs—swellings of stem tissue that store food and water. Cattleyas can also be propagated from seed, but it may take several years for the plants to flower. Scales, mealybugs, spider mites and virus are the major concerns in growing cattleyas.

—

Chenille plant see *Acalypha*
Chinese lantern see *Abutilon*
Christmas cactus see *Schlumbergera*

—

Chrysanthemum (kri-SAN-the-mum)

Genus of annuals or perennials, some species of which make good houseplants. The flowers are often, but not always, daisylike; foliage varies with the species and is often lobed or deeply cut.

Selected species and varieties. *C.* × *morifolium,* florist's chrysanthemum, varies in height from 1 to 2 feet when sold as a houseplant. Leaves are lobed, slightly hairy and up to 3 inches long. Flowers, which come in all colors except blue, also come in a variety of forms: single, anemone, pompon, incurved, reflexed, spider, decorative and spoon. Chrysanthemum flowers are made up of two parts: the center of the flower, or the disk, and the petal-like parts, called rays. Single flowers are daisylike and have up to five rows of rays surrounding a flat disk. Anemone flowers resemble the single flowers, except that the disk is hemispherical or tufted. Pompons have rays that curve inward to form a globular flower head and usually hide the disk. Incurved flowers have broad rays that curve inward and overlap to form a globular head; the disk is hidden. Reflexed flowers have rays that curve outward. Spider mums have long, narrow, drooping rays with tips that are hooked or coiled. Decorative flowers have narrow rays that curve outward and form a flatter flower head than the pompon. Spoon flowers have rays with spoon-shaped tips. Flowers also vary in size; some are button-sized and others are several inches across. Flowers last for about three weeks and may be forced into bloom by florists at any time of year.

Growing conditions. Chrysanthemums for the house are usually purchased when they are already in bud or in bloom, because it is difficult to force a mum into bloom indoors. If you want to try growing your own plants from scratch, propagate from stem cuttings, by division or from seed. Mums produce foliage when the days are more than 14½ hours long, and bloom when the days are less than 14½ hours long.

Place potted mums in a spot with average temperature, bright light and high humidity. The potting medium should be rich; keep it evenly moist at all times. Plants purchased in bloom will not require fertilizing. After a chrysanthemum has finished blooming, it may be discarded or transplanted into the garden. Hardiness of potted mums is variable, but they may survive, especially if they are transplanted outdoors in spring.

Chrysanthemums can attract aphids, mealybugs, spider mites, whiteflies, root knot nematodes and leaf miners, and can develop rust, leaf spot, root and stem rot, powdery mildew, botrytis blight and wilt.

—

Cigar flower see *Cuphea*

Cineraria see *Senecio*

—

Citrus (SIT-rus)

Genus of subtropical, fruit-bearing trees, some species of which are suitable for growing indoors. The leaves are thick, leathery and shiny; the stems are often spiny. The flowers are fragrant, white, lobed, up to 2 inches across, and appear most abundantly in spring and fall. Blooms usually appear in clusters and are followed by edible fruits that last on the plant for several months. Indoors, plants grow up to 4 feet tall.

Selected species and varieties. *C. limon,* lemon, has oblong to oval leaves and yellow, 3-inch, oval or round, tart fruit. 'Meyer', Meyer lemon, has round fruit. 'Ponderosa', wonder lemon, has orange-yellow, rough-skinned, 4½-inch fruit. *C. × limonia,* Otaheite orange, is a small, thornless plant with deep yellow to orange, 2-inch, sweet fruit. *C. reticulata,* mandarin orange, tangerine, has deep yellow-orange to orange-red fruit. *C. sinensis,*

CHRYSANTHEMUM × MORIFOLIUM

CITRUS SINENIS 'WASHINGTON'

CLERODENDRUM THOMSONIAE

CLIVIA MINIATA

orange, has round, orange, sweet-tasting, 4-inch fruit. 'Washington' is seedless and thick-skinned with a prominent navel. A related plant, × *Citrofortunella mitis,* formerly known as *Citrus mitis,* Panama orange, has orange, 1¼-inch, tart-tasting fruit. Another related plant, *Fortunella japonica,* kumquat, has round, deep orange, 1¼-inch, sweet-tasting fruit.

Growing conditions. Citrus grows best under high light, in warm temperature and high humidity. Pot in average, slightly acid growing medium, and allow the medium to dry out slightly between waterings. Fruits may drop if plants are under- or over-watered. Fertilize in early spring, in early summer and in late summer. When the plant is in bloom, shake it slightly to ensure pollination and the setting of fruit. Pinch growing tips to keep the plants compact. Stem cuttings taken between midsummer and late fall may be rooted. The major pests of citrus are scales, whiteflies, spider mites, rust and scab.

Clam shell orchid see *Epidendrum*

Clerodendrum (kler-o-DEN-drum)
Glory bower

Genus of tropical trees, shrubs and vines, several species of which are adaptable to growing indoors. Flowers are white, yellow, red, blue or violet; are tubular and five-lobed; and bloom in large clusters.

Selected species and varieties. *C. thomsoniae,* bleeding glory bower, is a vining plant with oval, quilted, shiny, papery, dark green, 5-inch leaves. Flowers are 1 to 2 inches across, and are red with white calyces—the petal-like structures that surround and protect the flower bud. They bloom most abundantly in spring and summer, but may bloom at other times if the heat and humidity are high enough. 'Delectum' has very large clusters of rose to magenta flowers. With pruning, plants can be kept at heights of 2 to 3 feet.

Growing conditions. Glory bower needs a room where temperature and humidity are high and light is bright. It can be grown in all-purpose potting medium that is kept evenly moist when the plant is growing and flowering, and allowed to dry slightly between waterings at other times. Fertilize every two weeks during spring and summer. After the plants have bloomed, cut them back to encourage new growth and flowering, and pinch off growing tips to keep the plants small and compact. Use the prunings to root new plants. Glory bower can be damaged by mealybugs, scales and leaf spot.

Clivia (KLY-vee-a)
Kaffir lily

Bulblike plant that has strap-shaped, narrow leaves and large clusters of tubular, colorful flowers that bloom in winter and spring on thick, leafless stems.

Selected species and varieties. *C. miniata* has 1½-foot-long, thick, waxy, arching and dark, shiny green leaves. Flowers are approximately 3 inches long and occur in clusters of 12 to 20. Flowers are salmon-red on the outside and yellow on the inside. 'Grandiflora' has broad, dark green leaves and very large, bright red flowers.

Growing conditions. Kaffir lily prefers a spot with average temperature and humidity and bright light. Pot plants in average growing medium, and allow the medium to dry out between waterings. After the plant has flowered, water only to keep it from wilting until new growth starts. Fertilize every six weeks in spring and summer. Plants grow and flower best if the roots are not disturbed, so repot them as infrequently as possible. Propagate kaffir lily by division after the plant has bloomed or from seed. Kaffir lily is free of insects and diseases.

—

COFFEA ARABICA

Coffea (KOF-ee-a)
Coffee

Tropical tree or shrub grown commercially as the source of coffee beans. The most important species is adaptable to growing indoors. Plants have clusters of funnel-shaped white flowers that are followed by small berries; both flowers and berries appear at the base of the leaves.

Selected species and varieties. *C. arabica,* common coffee, grows 1 to 4 feet high indoors. Plants have oval, dark green, shiny, 4-inch leaves and fragrant, five-lobed flowers in spring or summer. Berries that are bright red and ¼ to ½ inch across appear in winter.

Growing conditions. Coffee plant likes a warm spot with average to high humidity and bright light. The growing medium should be kept evenly moist at all times. From spring through fall, fertilize every two weeks; feed monthly the rest of the year. Cut plants back in the spring to keep them small and to encourage compact growth. New plants can be started from stem cuttings or from seed, but will not flower or fruit for three to four years. Coffee plants can attract aphids, mealybugs, scales and whiteflies, but are generally disease-free.

—

Coffee see *Coffea*

—

COLUMNEA MICROPHYLLA

Columnea (ko-LUM-nee-a)
Goldfish plant

Tropical plant in the gesneriad family that has trailing branches and is best used in a hanging basket. The flowers, which are 2 to 4 inches long, are tubular, two-lipped and when fully open look like goldfish. Flowers generally bloom in spring and summer but may appear off and on all year.

Selected species and varieties. *C. microphylla* has slender, hairy, reddish brown stems, and hairy, green or red, round, soft leaves up to ½ inch long, much smaller than other members of the genus. Flowers are 2½ inches long, and bright red with a yellow throat and markings at the base of the lower lip.

CONVALLARIA MAJALIS 'FORTUNEI'

CRINUM × POWELLII 'ALBUM'

Growing conditions. Goldfish plants do best in warm temperature, high humidity and bright light. They also grow well under 14 to 16 hours of fluorescent light a day. In winter, they prefer cool temperatures, which aid in setting flower buds. The growing medium should be rich and evenly moist. In the winter, if the plant is not growing or flowering, reduce watering and eliminate the fertilizer. After the plant has flowered, prune it back to encourage fullness and new growth. Pinch the growing tips to keep the plants small and bushy. Propagate from stem cuttings or by division. Mealybugs may attack, but goldfish plant is generally disease-free.

—

Convallaria (kon-va-LAR-ee-a)
Lily-of-the-valley

Perennial with rhizomatous roots that have growth buds called pips. Leaves grow from the base of the plant and surround bell-shaped, scalloped, nodding, fragrant, pink or white flowers that can be forced into bloom in winter or spring for use indoors.

Selected species and varieties. *C. majalis* grows 8 inches high and has two or three oblong, pointed leaves. The flowers appear along 8-inch stems. 'Aureo-variegata' has leaves variegated with yellow. 'Flora Plena' and 'Prolificans' have double flowers. 'Fortunei' has flowers and foliage that are larger than those of the species. 'Rosea' has pink flowers and is smaller and daintier than the species.

Growing conditions. Roots are available for sale in fall and winter, and should be potted in average growing medium that is kept evenly moist. Roots can also be dug from the garden in early spring and potted. Place pots in a cool area with average humidity and bright light. Fertilize every other week during growth and flowering. Plants will bloom in about four weeks. After a plant has bloomed, discard it, or withhold water until the foliage has turned brown, then move it to a shady spot in the garden. If plants are crowded, divide the pips at transplanting time. Lily-of-the-valley is not generally subject to insects or diseases indoors.

—

Copperleaf see *Acalypha*
Coralberry see *Aechmea; Ardisia*

—

Crinum (KRY-num)
Spider lily, crinum lily

Genus of tropical and subtropical plants that grow from bulbs, several species of which can be grown indoors. Leaves are strap- or sword-shaped and arching; flowers are trumpet-shaped and fragrant, and appear in clusters on top of thick, leafless stems. Blooms usually appear in summer and fall. Plants grow several feet high and wide, depending on the species.

Selected species and varieties. *C. bulbi-spermum* has narrow, 2-foot leaves and trumpetlike flowers that are 3 to 4 inches long and 1 inch wide, blooming in clusters on 2-foot stems. Blooms are white, brushed with red on the inside. 'Alba' has white flowers. 'Roseum' has pink flowers. *C. moorei* is a larger plant with broader leaves. The flowers are rose-red, except for 'Album', which has white flowers, and 'Roseum', which has pink flowers. *C. × powellii,* a hybrid between the two crinums above, is the size of *C. moorei,* with leaves growing 3 to 4 feet long, and has 4- to 6-inch red flowers on 3-foot stems. 'Album' has white flowers; the blooms of 'Roseum' are pink.

Growing conditions. Place tubs or pots of crinums in a room with average temperature and humidity and direct light. The growing medium should be kept evenly moist, and fertilizer should be applied monthly when the plant is growing or flowering. After the blooms have faded, reduce watering, supplying only enough moisture to keep the plant from wilting. The following spring, repot if necessary and increase watering. Bulbs produce offsets, which can be removed and repotted to increase the number of plants. Crinum is rarely bothered by insects, but may be subject to leaf spot and virus diseases.

▬

Crocus (KRO-kus)

Spring- or fall-flowering bulb that can be forced into bloom during the winter for growing indoors. The leaves are thin, striped and grassy; flowers, which are six-petaled and cup-shaped, are white, yellow, lilac or purple.

Selected species and varieties. *C. vernus,* Dutch crocus, has been widely hybridized, and large-flowered varieties growing up to 6 inches tall are available. Some flowers have solid colors; others are striped or marked with contrasting colors on the inside of the petals.

Growing conditions. Crocus requires a cold treatment before it will flower. You can purchase bulbs that have been prechilled, in which case all you need to do is pot them and place them in the house. If you buy bulbs that have not been prechilled, pot them in the fall and place them outdoors, either buried in the ground or in a cold frame, for three to four months before moving them indoors. Pots should not be allowed to freeze. Alternatively, bulbs can be potted and placed in the refrigerator for artificial chilling. Grow in an all-purpose, well-drained growing medium; do not fertilize. After chilling, potted plants should be placed in bright light in a cool room with average humidity. Keep plants evenly moist. Crocus will bloom within two weeks. After the blooms have faded, the bulbs should be discarded; they will not successfully rebloom indoors. Crocus suffers from few insects and few diseases when grown as a houseplant.

▬

Crossandra (kro-SAN-dra)
Firecracker flower

Rounded, shrubby plant that adapts well to indoor growing. It has oval or lance-shaped foliage and tubular flowers that open into five round lobes. Blooms appear in clusters at the ends of the branches.

CROCUS VERNUS

CROSSANDRA INFUNDIBULIFORMIS

CUPHEA IGNEA

CYCLAMEN PERSICUM

Selected species and varieties. *C. infundibuliformis* has shiny, wavy-edged, 2- to 5-inch leaves that clothe 12-inch plants. The flowers, which appear primarily in spring and summer, are bright orange or salmon, each 1¼ inches across. Clusters measure up to 6 inches wide.

Growing conditions. Firecracker flower needs bright light, a warm room and high humidity; if humidity is too low, leaves will curl and plants will not flower. The potting medium should be extra rich and kept evenly moist at all times during the growth and flowering periods. Fertilize every two weeks when the plant is growing or flowering. During fall and winter, allow the medium to dry out slightly between waterings, and do not fertilize. If plants become leggy, the growing tips can be pinched to encourage compactness. Take cuttings to root new plants at any time of year, or start new plants from seed. Spider mites can damage firecracker flower, but few if any diseases attack it.

Crown-of-thorns see *Euphorbia*

Cuphea (KEW-fee-a)

Genus of annuals, perennials and shrubs, several species of which are commonly grown indoors. The flowers are tubular and bloom continuously.

Selected species and varieties. *C. ignea,* sometimes designated *C. platycentra,* cigar flower, firecracker plant, has slender stems and oblong to lance-shaped leaves that are 1 to 3 inches long. The flowers are 1 inch long and have a bright red tube with a tip of violet or black with white, and look like a lit cigar or a firecracker. Stems are 12 to 18 inches long and the plants are suitable for growing in hanging baskets.

Growing conditions. Set cigar flower in a room where temperature and humidity are average and light is direct. Keep the growing medium evenly moist, and fertilize every two weeks. New plants may be started from seed or from stem cuttings taken at any time. Cigar flower can be attacked by scales, botrytis blight, leaf spot and root rot.

Cyclamen (SIK-la-men or SY-kla-men)
Persian violet

Tuberous perennial, one species of which is grown as a houseplant. Leaves form at the base of the plant, are heart-shaped, and are marbled in light green, gray or silver on the upper surfaces. The flowers are held high above the foliage. They are nodding, and their petals sweep upward like butterfly wings.

Selected species and varieties. *C. persicum,* florist's cyclamen, generally grows 8 to 10 inches tall, but miniature varieties grow only 4 to 6 inches high. The leaves grow up to 5½ inches across. The flowers are up to 2 inches long and are white, pink, rose, red, magenta, lavender or purple, with a purplish blotch at the base. Some varieties have frilled petals. The species has fragrant flowers; the newer F_1 hybrids have no scent.

Growing conditions. Cyclamen needs cool temperature, high humidity and bright light to survive in the house. The potting medium must be very rich and moist at all times. Do not allow water to fall into the crown of the plant during watering, as this may cause crown rot; bottom watering may help prevent this problem. When plants are growing, fertilize once a month; when they are blooming, fertilize every two weeks. After a cyclamen has ceased blooming, gradually withhold water and stop fertilizing. When the foliage has turned yellow, let the plant dry out and store it in its pot in a dark, 45° F area for tree months. Then bring it back into the house and start watering to encourage new growth. Plants generally flower in winter and spring and rest over the summer when temperatures are high. If the tubers are large, they may be divided in early fall before new growth starts. Cyclamen may also be grown from seed. Older varieties need 12 to 15 months to produce blooming plants; newer F_1 hybrids will bloom in seven to eight months. Botrytis blight, spider and cyclamen mites, and thrips may attack cyclamen.

CYMBIDIUM HYBRID

Cymbidium (sim-BID-ee-um)

Orchid that has long, narrow, leathery leaves. The flowers are 2 to 4 inches across and have five petals of equal size and central, lobed lips that are often of contrasting colors. Blooms appear from fall through spring in spikes of 10 to 30 flowers.

Selected species and varieties. There are large numbers of *Cymbidium* species and complex hybrids that grow from 1 to 2 feet tall and have flowers of white, pink, yellow, green, maroon, bronze and mahogany. Miniature cymbidiums grow about 12 inches high and are better suited to growing as houseplants. *C. devonianum* is one of the most common miniature species and has flowers of olive green to creamy yellow. There is also a large number of miniature hybrids.

Growing conditions. To be grown as houseplants, cymbidiums must have cool to average temperature, high humidity and bright light. Plants will not set flower buds unless the temperature is low (45° to 50° F) in fall. Use a growing medium made for orchids, and keep it evenly moist. Fertilize monthly using a complete fertilizer. Plants benefit from being moved outdoors in the summer and fall, or into a cool greenhouse when not in bloom. Cymbidiums are propagated by division of the rhizomes and stems in spring or summer. The stems are made up of water- and food-storage structures called pseudobulbs. Ensure that there are three or four pseudobulbs in each division. Cymbidiums may also be grown from seed. Cymbidiums may be attacked by mealybugs, spider mites, scales and virus diseases.

Daffodil see *Narcissus*
Dancing-lady orchid see *Oncidium*

DAPHNE ODORA

Daphne (DAF-nee)

Genus of evergreen trees and shrubs, one species of which is grown as a houseplant. Plants are compact, and have clusters of fragrant, bell-shaped, four-petaled flowers that bloom at the branch tips.

Selected species and varieties. *D. odora,* winter daphne, grows 1 to 2 feet tall as a houseplant. Leaves are 2 to 3 inches long, oblong, narrow, shiny and leathery. Flowers are highly fragrant, white, pink, red or purple, and bloom in fall and winter.

Growing conditions. Grow winter daphne in a cool room where humidity is average and light is bright. The potting medium should be allowed to dry slightly between waterings. Fertilize once in the spring with a fertilizer designed for acid-loving plants. After the plant has flowered, it can be cut back to keep it compact. Daphne can be propagated by cuttings, by layering or from seed. Daphne can develop leaf spot and stem rot and may attract aphids, mealybugs and scales.

Dauphin violet see *Streptocarpus*

Dendrobium (den-DRO-bee-um)

Orchid that has a broad range of species. Some have flat, thin leaves; others have thick, leathery leaves. Flowers appear in sprays or clusters, with individual flowers 1 to 3 inches across, and often twisted or curled.

Selected species and varieties. *D. aggregatum* has drooping clusters of 1½- to 2-inch yellow flowers and blooms in spring. It grows only a few inches high. *D. densiflorum* has 2-inch yellow or orange flowers that bloom on 1½ foot stems in spring. *D. fimbriatum oculatum* has 2- to 3-inch orange-yellow flowers that bloom on 4-foot stems in spring; the base of the flower lip is fringed and its center is blotched in maroon. *D. nobile* has 3-inch, fragrant, rose-lilac or white flowers that bloom on 2- to 3-foot stems in winter and spring. *D. pierardii* has 2-inch flowers that are white with purple tips and yellow centers. Many dendrobium hybrids have flowers of white, rose, yellow, magenta or purple; different hybrids bloom at different times of year. Most plants have long, slender canes; some grow upright while others do well in hanging baskets.

Growing conditions. Dendrobiums like bright to direct light, average to warm temperature and high humidity. The growing medium should be one especially made for orchids, with a high bark content. Many dendrobiums can be grown on slabs of tree fern. When plants are flowering, keep the medium evenly moist and fertilize monthly with a complete fertilizer; at other times, allow the medium to dry slightly between waterings. If plants do not set flower buds, lowering the temperature may help; eliminating fertilizer and reducing the amount of water may also help. Moving dendrobiums into a cool greenhouse or outdoors in summer and fall may aid flowering; once the plants are in flower, they may be moved indoors. Dendrobiums do not like having their roots disturbed, so repot as infrequently as possible. It is normal for some dendrobiums to lose

DENDROBIUM PIERARDII

some of their leaves during the fall and winter. The stems are made up of water- and food-storing tissue called pseudobulbs; when dividing dendrobiums, be sure that each division contains three to six pseudobulbs. Dendrobiums that have canelike stems may also be propagated by stem cuttings, and all can be propagated from seed. Dendrobiums may be susceptible to mealybugs, spider mites, scales and virus diseases.

—

Easter lily see *Lilium*

—

Echeveria (ek-e-VEER-ee-a)
Hen-and-chickens

Large genus of succulent plants, many of which are adapted to indoor growing. The leaves generally appear in rounded rosettes. Spikes of bell-shaped flowers appear between the leaves. The plant takes its common name from the many small plantlets that form around the base of the mother plant.

Selected species and varieties. *E. derenbergii,* painted lady, has thick, rounded, spoon-shaped leaves, with 40 or 70 leaves in a tight, 4- to 6-inch rosette. The leaves are bluish green, and often tipped in red. The flowers are red and yellow and bloom on 4-inch stems in winter and spring. *E. setosa,* firecracker plant, has 80 to 175 oblong, hairy leaves with rounded and pointed tips. The red flowers are tipped in yellow and bloom on a 4- to 6-inch stem in spring or summer.

Growing conditions. Grow hen-and-chickens in a room where temperature is average, humidity is average and light is direct. Use an average to sandy potting medium, and allow it to dry out between waterings. In winter, water only to keep the plant from shriveling. Fertilize monthly in spring and summer. To increase the number of plants, remove and repot the small plantlets that form around the base of the mother plant. Plants may be subject to attack by scales, leaf spot and root rot.

—

Egyptian star see *Pentas*

—

Epidendrum (ep-i-DEN-drum)
Buttonhole orchid

Large genus of orchids, some of which can be grown as houseplants. There are two types of epidendrums: one has sprawling, grassy canes; the other has hard pseudobulbs and waxy, strap-shaped leaves, and is sometimes designated *Encyclia.* The flowers bloom in sprays; individual flower shape varies with the species and some are fragrant.

Selected species and varieties. *E. cochleatum,* clam shell orchid, grows 12 inches high in an erect, leafy habit from pseudobulbs. The flowers are slightly fragrant and dark maroon and yellow. There is a large lip at the top of the flower and five narrow petals hanging down below it; compared with other

ECHEVERIA SETOSA

EPIDENDRUM RADICANS

EPIPHYLLUM HYBRID

EPISCIA DIANTHIFLORA

orchids, it looks as if it were upside down. Plants bloom most abundantly in winter and early spring. *E. radicans* grows to 2 feet high indoors and has long canes, along the length of which many thin roots emerge and develop into plants. The flowers are 1 to 1½ inches across, have a fringed yellow lip, have five orange to brown petals and may bloom at any time of year. Hybrids are available in many colors.

Growing conditions. Buttonhole orchids prefer direct or bright light, high humidity and cool to average temperature. Grow in a potting mix made for orchids, or a standard soilless mix with additional unmilled sphagnum moss, fir or redwood bark, or osmunda fiber. Keep the medium evenly moist when the plant is growing and blooming; at other times, allow it to dry out between waterings. Fertilize monthly when the plant is growing or flowering. Use a complete fertilizer. The species with canes can be trained on tree-fern poles or may be staked. Depending on the species, propagate either by dividing the pseudobulbs or the canes, or by removing the plantlets that form on the canes. Scales, mealybugs, spider mites and virus diseases may attack.

Epiphyllum (ep-i-FY-lum)
Orchid cactus

A cactus that is known as a jungle cactus because it requires higher humidity, more water and richer soil than a desert cactus. The branches are flat, lobed and arching. The flowers are large, tubular and fragrant, and have flaring petals that open into a cup or funnel shape to reveal showy stamens. Some species have flowers that open only at night; others are day-blooming.

Selected species and varieties. *Epiphyllum* hybrids have showy flowers of white, yellow, pink, red, blue or purple, many of which bloom in winter; the others, in spring. The flowers are luminescent and may be up to 7 inches long. Because of its arching branches, orchid cactus is suited to a hanging basket.

Growing conditions. Grow orchid cactus where temperature and humidity are average and light is bright. Grow in cool temperatures to promote flowering. The potting medium should be slightly rich. In winter, when temperatures are lower, allow the medium to dry slightly between waterings. When flower buds form, increase watering so that the medium is kept evenly moist. If flower buds drop, the plant is not receiving enough water. Avoid moving the plant after flower buds have formed, since any disturbance may cause the buds to drop. After the plant has flowered, pinch it back to keep it compact and start monthly fertilizing, stopping in fall. The cuttings can be used to root new plants. Orchid cactus may be attacked by spider mites and may develop rot and wilt diseases.

Episcia (e-PIS-ee-a)
Carpet plant

Tropical plant in the gesneriad family that adapts to the indoors. The plant has long, slender stems that produce small plantlets at their ends. The leaves are

2 to 5 inches across, oval and hairy. The flowers are 1 to 1½ inches long, tubular to bell-shaped, five-lobed, and bloom in spring and summer. Because the long stems droop gracefully, carpet plant makes an excellent display in a hanging basket.

Selected species and varieties. *E. cupreata,* flame violet, has 2- to 5-inch wrinkled leaves that are green, reddish green, copper or marked with silver. The blooms are dark red and have yellow undersides with red spots. 'Chocolate Velour' has very hairy, heavily textured dark brown to black leaves. The leaves of 'Metallica' have metallic pink margins and bands of pale green in the center. 'Variegata' has leaves with a silver pattern on the center. *E. dianthiflora,* lace flower vine, has soft, hairy, 1½-inch green leaves that are often red-veined and white flowers. *E. lilacina* has 4-inch, quilted leaves that are green, reddish green or bronze, often with rose-purple undersides. The flowers are lavender and have yellow throats. *E. reptans,* flame violet, has 5-inch, quilted, dark green leaves that have pale green or silver midribs. The flowers are dark red, pink inside the tube and fringed.

Growing conditions. Grow carpet plant in a warm, humid room where light is bright. The growing medium should be extra rich and evenly moist. Do not allow cold water to touch the leaves or they may spot. Fertilize monthly during spring and summer. After the plant flowers, cut it back to encourage new growth and pinch the new growth to encourage fullness. New plants can be propagated by rooting the plantlets that form at the ends of the stems or from stem cuttings. Carpet plant is vulnerable to attack by spider mites, whiteflies, mealybugs and botrytis blight.

EUCHARIS GRANDIFLORA

Eucharis (YEW-ka-ris)

Bulb that produces broad leaves from the base of the plant and clusters of white flowers atop thick, leafless 12- to 24-inch stems.

Selected species and varieties. *E. grandiflora,* Amazon lily, has broad, shiny leaves that are 1 foot long. The clusters have three to six fragrant, 2- to 3-inch flaring flowers that can be forced to bloom at any time of year.

Growing conditions. Grow Amazon lily in a warm room where humidity is high and light is bright. Pot in well-drained, coarse growing medium so the tip of the bulb is just below the surface of the medium. Water heavily until the foliage is fully grown, then withhold water until the leaves droop, and place the plant in a cool room for two to three weeks to induce flower buds. Then return the plant to its normal growing conditions and resume heavy watering. After the plant has bloomed, reduce watering until the foliage has died down. Place the plant in a cool spot for several months to rest, and then start the process over again. Fertilize monthly when the plant is growing. Propagate by removing the offset bulbs that form at the base of the plant or from seed. Amazon lily can be pestered by mealybugs and scales and is susceptible to botrytis blight.

EUPHORBIA MILII

EUPHORBIA PULCHERRIMA

Euphorbia (yew-FOR-bee-a)
Spurge

Very large genus of succulent plants, many of which have tiny flowers that are surrounded by colorful bracts. Leaves and stems, when broken, ooze a milky sap that may cause a skin rash.

Selected species and varieties. *E. fulgens,* scarlet plume, has slender arching or drooping branches that grow to 2 feet long. The leaves are narrow, lance-shaped and 2 to 4 inches long; the flowers are surrounded by orange-red, rounded bracts and bloom in winter. *E. milii,* crown-of-thorns, is a shrubby plant that grows 1 to 3 feet tall. The stems are brown and very spiny. The leaves are dull green and appear sparsely, mostly on the new growth; they are oval to spoon-shaped and grow to 2½ inches long. The flowers are surrounded by red or yellow bracts that appear in summer. *E. pulcherrima,* poinsettia, grows 6 inches to 4 feet tall. The leaves are 4 to 7 inches long, toothed or lobed, and dull green. The flowers are surrounded in winter by showy bracts of white, pink, red, or mottled combinations of the three colors.

Growing conditions. All spurges are grown in direct light. Scarlet plume prefers warm temperature and high humidity. Crown-of-thorns is grown at average to warm temperature and average humidity. Poinsettia prefers average temperature when it is growing and cool to average temperatures when it is flowering, and average humidity. Grow all in a well-drained, soilless medium. Scarlet plume and crown-of-thorns should be watered when the surface of the medium dries out; poinsettias should be kept evenly moist at all times. Fertilize scarlet plume and crown-of-thorns every two weeks from spring through fall. Fertilize poinsettia every month from late spring until fall or early winter when the bracts have fully developed their color. Prune crown-of-thorns and scarlet plume in early spring to keep them compact. Poinsettias are increased by stem cuttings; scarlet plume and crown-of-thorns are propagated by stem cuttings or from seed.

Poinsettias purchased for the winter holidays can be grown indoors until the bracts drop in the spring. Then, cut the plants back and either continue to grow the original plant or use the prunings for rooting new plants. Plants benefit from being placed outdoors in partial sun during the summer and can be pinched to keep them compact. Move plants back indoors about September 1. To force them to bloom for the holidays, shade them with black cloth, with a box that covers the entire plant, or by putting the plant in a closet each night. Shade the plants for 15 hours each night for about six weeks. Depending on the variety, they will be in bloom in 8½ to 11 weeks after the start of the shading process.

Spurge is susceptible to attack by whiteflies, spider mites, aphids, mealybugs, botrytis blight, and root and stem rot.

Exacum (EK-sa-kum)

Shrubby plant that has small, four- to five-lobed, flaring flowers.

Selected species and varieties. *E. affine,* German violet, Persian violet, is a multibranched plant that can grow up to 2 feet high, but is usually 6 to 12 inches tall. Leaves are light green, oval, waxy and ½ to 1 inch long. Flowers are white, blue or lavender, star-shaped, fragrant and ½ inch across, with yellow eyes and stamens. Plants are generally grown to bloom in fall and winter, but can be grown to flower anytime. 'Blythe Spirit' has white flowers. 'Midget' has light violet-blue or white flowers.

Growing conditions. Grow German violet in a warm room with bright light and high humidity. The growing medium should be extra rich and evenly moist at all times. Fertilize every two weeks. To extend the blooming period, remove flowers as they fade. After the plant has finished flowering, it will die and should be discarded. Propagate from seed sown in the spring for fall and winter bloom, or from stem cuttings taken before the plant is discarded. German violet is not prone to attack by insects or diseases.

—

Firecracker flower see *Crossandra*

Firecracker plant see *Cuphea; Echeveria*

Flame-of-the-woods see *Ixora*

Flame violet see *Episcia*

Flamingo flower see *Anthurium*

Flamingo lily see *Anthurium*

Flaming-sword see *Vriesea*

Flowering maple see *Abutilon*

Foolproof plant see *Billbergia*

Four-leaf clover see *Oxalis*

—

Freesia (FREE-zha)

Corm that produces wiry, arching spikes of highly fragrant, funnel-shaped flowers that appear on the upper sides of the flowering stem. Plants produce only a few linear leaves.

Selected species and varieties. *F. × hybrida* is a group of hybrids that have 2-inch single or double flowers of white, yellow, orange, red, bronze, lavender, blue, purple or pink. Plants may be brought into flower at any time of year, but are usually grown for winter and spring bloom.

Growing conditions. Grow freesia in a cool room with direct light and average humidity. Plant corms 1 inch deep in well-drained, soilless medium. Keep the medium barely moist when the plant is growing; as soon as buds form and until the flowers fade, keep the medium constantly moist. Fertilize monthly when the plant is in bud or is flowering. The corms will flower three to four months after they are planted; plants will need to be staked. After plants have bloomed, decrease watering, allow the foliage to turn brown, remove the corms from the pot and store them at 45° F in a dark place until the following season; then replant. Freesia can also be propagated from seed. Freesia is not susceptible to insects or diseases.

—

Friendship plant see *Billbergia*

EXACUM AFFINE

FREESIA × HYBRIDA

FUCHSIA × HYBRIDA

Fuchsia (FEW-sha)
Lady's-eardrops

Genus of upright and trailing plants with delicate, drooping flowers that are shaped like hoop skirts. The flowers are usually two-toned and have long, showy stamens.

Selected species and varieties. *F. × hybrida* is a group of hybrids that have 1- to 3-foot trailing stems, which make them ideal for hanging baskets. The leaves are oval and 4 inches long. The flowers are in combinations of white, pink, magenta, rose, red and purple. Flowers may appear all year, but bloom most abundantly from midspring to midfall.

Growing conditions. Grow fuchsia in a cool room with limited light and average to high humidity. The growing medium should be rich and well drained. Keep the medium evenly moist from spring through fall; in winter, allow the medium to dry slightly between waterings. Fertilize monthly during spring and summer. Plants benefit from being placed outdoors in a shaded spot during the summer. After a plant has flowered, cut the branches back to encourage new and compact growth, and pinch the growing tips regularly to further encourage compactness. Fuchsia is propagated from stem cuttings or from seed. Spider mites, aphids, mealybugs, whiteflies and scales may attack fuchsia; plants are prone to botrytis blight, leaf spot and root rot.

—

Gardenia (gar-DEEN-ya)

Evergreen or deciduous tree or shrub that has white or yellow, heavily fragrant, single or double flowers. One species is commonly grown as a houseplant.

Selected species and varieties. *G. jasminoides,* Cape jasmine, is an evergreen that grows to 1 to 3 feet high indoors. The leaves are oval to lance-shaped, thick, glossy, dark green and 4 to 6 inches long. The flowers are waxy, double, white and 3 inches across. Flowers appear most abundantly in winter and spring. 'Prostrata' is a low-growing variety. 'Fortuniana' has 4-inch double flowers.

Growing conditions. Cape jasmine prefers a warm room, direct light and high humidity. For flower buds to set, the night temperature must be at least 60° F. Grow in soilless, acidic, well-drained medium, and fertilize monthly with a plant food for acid-loving plants. Pinch plants to encourage branching; stop pinching five months before the desired bloom date. If winter bloom is desired, remove any flower buds that form before late September. Propagate from stem cuttings. Flower buds will drop if the air is too dry, if the plant is in a draft, if it is improperly watered or if it receives insufficient light. If new growth turns yellow, it is often a sign of iron chlorosis; ensure that the pH is acidic and treat with iron sulfate.

Cape jasmine is attacked by aphids, mealybugs, spider mites and thrips, and is subject to canker and leaf spot diseases.

—

Garland flower see *Hedychium*

GARDENIA JASMINOIDES

Gazania (ga-ZAY-nee-a)

Genus of annuals or perennials, one species of which is grown as a houseplant. The leaves grow in basal rosettes; the flowers are daisylike and bloom on leafless stems.

Selected species and varieties. *G. rigens,* treasure flower, has lance-shaped to oval leaves that grow 3 to 3½ inches long. The undersides of the leaves are white and hairy; the upper surfaces are dark green. The flowers are 2½ to 3 inches across, white, cream, yellow, gold, pink, bronze or orange, and bloom on 4- to 10-inch stems. Some flowers have dark centers; others have a dark, contrasting band at the center of the petals. The flowers close at night and on cloudy days. Plants may bloom year round indoors. 'Chansonette' grows 10 inches high and has flowers of cream, yellow, orange or pink. 'Mini-star' grows 8 inches high and has white, yellow or tangerine flowers.

Growing conditions. Treasure flower should be grown where temperature is cool to average, light is direct and humidity is average. Plant in well-drained medium and allow the medium to dry out between waterings. Fertilize monthly. Remove faded flowers to encourage further bloom. Treasure flower is propagated from seed or by division. It is resistant to attack by insects but can develop crown rot.

GAZANIA RIGENS 'MINI-STAR TANGERINE'

Geranium see *Pelargonium*

Gerbera (jer-BEER-a)

Genus of perennials, one species of which is commonly grown as a houseplant. The leaves grow in a basal rosette; the flowers are daisylike and bloom singly on thick, leafless stems.

Selected species and varieties. *G. Jamesonii,* Transvaal daisy, has oblong, lobed or divided, hairy leaves that grow up to 10 inches long. The flowers are single or semidouble, 4 inches across, and white, yellow, salmon, pink, red or orange. Flowering stems reach heights of 18 to 24 inches. Transvaal daisy may flower at any time of year, and is commonly grown for winter and spring bloom. Each bloom may last for four weeks. 'Happipot' grows 8 to 10 inches high and is available in a number of colors.

Growing conditions. Transvaal daisy grows well in a wide range of temperatures, but needs direct light. Grow in rich, soilless, well-drained medium. The medium should be kept evenly moist when the plant is growing or flowering, and allowed to dry slightly between waterings at other times. Fertilize monthly during spring and summer. Transvaal daisy is propagated from cuttings or from seed. Ensure that the plant's crown is set above the medium or crown rot may occur. Transvaal daisy is also subject to mildew and is attacked by spider and cyclamen mites, mealybugs, thrips, root knot nematodes and whiteflies.

GERBERA JAMESONII

German violet see *Exacum*
Ginger lily see *Hedychium*

GLORIOSA SUPERBA

Gloriosa (glor-ee-O-sa)
Gloriosa lily

Tuberous, vining perennial that can be grown as a houseplant. The flowers are yellow, red or purple, and have wavy or crisped margins.

Selected species and varieties. *G. superba* has weak stems that grow 3 to 5 feet tall. The leaves are oblong to lance-shaped and 4 to 6 inches long. The flowers are drooping, green at first, then yellow with red tips, then change to solid red, and have narrow, 3-inch, reflexed petals. 'Lutea' has clear yellow flowers. Plants bloom in late summer and fall.

Growing conditions. Grow gloriosa lily where temperature is warm, humidity is high and light is direct. Plant in soilless, well-drained medium, and keep it evenly moist when the plant is growing or flowering. Fertilize every two weeks during the growing and flowering period. Plants should be staked or tied to a trellis. Plant tubers 3 inches deep in winter for bloom the following summer and fall. After the plants have finished blooming, withhold water and allow them to go dormant. Start watering again the following winter. Propagate gloriosa lily by division of the tubers, by offsets or from seed. Gloriosa lily is immune to attack by insects and diseases.

—

Glory bower see *Clerodendrum*

Glory bush see *Tibouchina*

Gloxinia see *Sinningia*

Golden trumpet see *Allamanda*

Goldfish plant see *Columnea*

Grape hyacinth see *Muscari*

Guernsey lily see *Nerine*

—

GUZMANIA LINGULATA

Guzmania (guz-MAY-nee-a)

A member of the bromeliad family having stiff leaves that grow in basal rosettes. Flowers are white or yellow, are surrounded by colorful bracts and bloom in spikes in the winter.

Selected species and varieties. *G. lingulata* grows 12 inches high and has narrow, arching, metallic green leaves that grow 18 inches long. There is a cuplike space at the base of the leaves. The flowers are white and are surrounded by leathery pink or red outer bracts and waxy orange-red inner bracts tipped with white or yellow. 'Major', sometimes designated as 'Broadview', has leaves that are red at the base. The flowers are white and surrounded by long, recurving, shiny, leathery, bright red bracts. 'Minor' has thin, leathery, strap-shaped, yellow-green leaves that have a thin, vertical maroon stripe. The bracts are orange-red around white flowers.

Growing conditions. Grow guzmania in a warm room with average humidity and indirect light. Plant in a rich, well-drained, soilless medium, and keep it evenly moist. Ensure that there is always water in the cup at the base of the plant. Fertilize monthly with quarter-strength liquid fertilizer. Propagate from offshoots that appear at the base of the plant. Guzmania is generally not subject to attack by insects or diseases, but occasionally scales or crown rot may attack.

Haemanthus (he-MAN-thus)
Blood lily

Bulb that has broad leaves at the base of the plant and dense, globe-shaped clusters of flowers that bloom at the top of a thick, leafless stem.

Selected species and varieties. *H. multiflorus* has three to four leaves, each 12 to 18 inches long and 6 inches wide. Flowers are blood red, 1 inch long, tubular and bloom in clusters 6 to 12 inches across on 18-inch stems. There can be up to 100 flowers in the cluster, and each has prominent yellow stamens. Plants bloom in summer and fall; flowers are followed by scarlet berries.

Growing conditions. Grow blood lily in a cool room with direct light and average to high humidity. Plant bulbs with the tip just above the surface of a well-drained, soilless medium, and keep it evenly moist during growth and flowering. Fertilize monthly when the plant is growing or flowering. After the flowers have bloomed, withhold water and allow the foliage to turn brown. Store the bulbs over the winter in the pot, and resume watering in early spring. Propagate by removing the bulblets that form around the base of the mother bulb. Blood lily may be attacked by mealybugs and scales and is prone to botrytis blight and leaf spot.

Hedychium (he-DIK-ee-um)
Ginger lily

Tropical perennial that grows from thick rhizomes. The stems are 4 feet long and leafy; the flowers are showy, fragrant and tubular, and bloom in spikes or clusters at the tops of the stems in spring and summer.

Selected species and varieties. *H. coronarium,* garland flower, white ginger, has leaves that are 2 feet long, 5 inches wide and silver on the undersides. The flowers are pure white and bloom in rounded clusters. The flowers are often used to make Hawaiian leis. *H. flavescens,* yellow ginger, has lance-shaped, 18-inch leaves and rounded clusters of 4- to 5-inch flowers that are yellow with a darker base. *H. gardneranum,* Kahili ginger, has 18-inch leaves that are white on the undersides when they are young. Flower spikes are loose, 12 to 18 inches long and contain yellow flowers that have long, conspicuous, red stamens.

Growing conditions. Ginger lily prefers warm temperature, bright light and average to high humidity. Grow it in an extra-rich, soilless medium and keep it constantly wet. Fertilize monthly. Propagate by dividing the rhizomes. Ginger lily is susceptible to mealybugs and scales.

Heliotrope see *Heliotropium*

HAEMANTHUS MULTIFLORUS

HEDYCHIUM GARDNERANUM

HELIOTROPIUM ARBORESCENS

HETEROCENTRON ELEGANS

Heliotropium (he-lee-o-TRO-pee-um)
Heliotrope

Genus of perennials and shrubs, one species of which is grown as a houseplant. The flowers are blue, purple, pink or white, five-lobed and tiny, and bloom year round indoors.

Selected species and varieties. *H. arborescens* grows 1 to 4 feet indoors, depending on how it is pruned. It has oblong to lance-shaped, 1- to 3-inch, hairy, wrinkled leaves. The flowers are blue, purple or white, heavily fragrant, soft-textured, ¼ inch long and bloom in large clusters 3 to 6 inches across.

Growing conditions. Grow heliotrope in a warm room with direct or bright light and average humidity. The growing medium should be rich, soilless and well drained, and should be kept evenly moist. Fertilize every two weeks. To keep plants small and compact, prune them back in the fall. Propagate by cuttings or from seed at any time. Heliotrope can be attacked by aphids, mealybugs, spider mites and whiteflies, and is susceptible to botrytis blight, leaf spot and rust.

—

Hen-and-chickens see *Echeveria*

—

Heterocentron (het-e-ro-KEN-tron)

Genus of perennials and shrubs, one species of which is grown as a houseplant. It has small leaves with three to 15 prominent veins and white, pink or purple flowers.

Selected species and varieties. *H. elegans,* formerly designated *Schizocentron elegans,* Spanish-shawl, is a trailing plant with slender, reddish stems. Because of its growth habit, it is suitable for a hanging basket. The leaves are oval to diamond-shaped, ¼ to ½ inch long, dark green and slightly hairy. The flowers are satiny, four-petaled, rosy purple, 1 inch across and bloom in summer.

Growing conditions. Grow Spanish-shawl in average temperature, bright light and high humidity. Grow in a rich medium and keep it evenly moist. Fertilize monthly. Propagate from stem cuttings or from seed. Insects and diseases are uncommon.

—

Hibiscus (hy-BIS-kus)

Genus of perennials, trees and shrubs, one species of which is grown as a houseplant. The flowers, which bloom in the leaf axils, are trumpet-shaped, with five lobes or petals, and a long, prominent projection emerging from the center of the flower.

Selected species and varieties. *H. rosa-sinensis,* Chinese hibiscus, will grow to 5 feet indoors but is best if pruned to 3 feet. The leaves are 3 to 6 inches long, oval to heart-shaped, glossy and toothed. The flowers are 2 to 5 inches across, single or double, papery, white, cream, salmon, pink, red, yellow or orange, and usually have a dark center. Each flower lasts only one day, but is quickly replaced by another. Plants will flower year round under proper growing conditions, but blooming is most abundant in summer and fall.

Growing conditions. Grow Chinese hibiscus in a warm room where light is direct and humidity is average to high. Plant in well-drained, soilless medium that is kept evenly moist. Fertilize monthly in fall and winter and every two weeks in spring and summer. Prune plants in the spring if they become too tall, and to encourage compact growth. Propagate from stem cuttings; plants may also be grown from seed but will not come true to variety or color. Chinese hibiscus is damaged by aphids, scales, mealybugs, whiteflies, leaf spot and stem rot.

Hindu rope see *Hoya*

Hippeastrum (hip-ee-AS-trum)
Amaryllis

Tropical bulb that has narrow to strap-shaped leaves that grow from the base of the plant. Flower clusters have multiple blooms on the tops of thick, leafless, hollow stems.

Selected species and varieties. *Hippeastrum* hybrids are a large group of plants with trumpet-shaped, 4- to 8- inch flowers that range in color from white to pink, orange, yellow and red. Some blooms are patterned or striped, and up to four blooms appear on each 18-inch stem. Plants bloom in winter or spring. The leaves may appear with or after the flowers.

Growing conditions. Grow amaryllis in a warm room in direct light and high humidity. Plant bulbs half-extending above a rich, well-drained, soilless medium. Plant one bulb per pot, with 1 inch between the pot rim and the bulb. Water the plant after potting, and do not water it again until growth starts. Then keep the medium evenly moist during growth and flowering. Fertilize every two weeks from the time growth starts until midsummer, when the foliage will turn yellow and die down. Keep plants dry and store them in a cool, dark area at 50° F until four to six weeks before flowers are desired. Then the plants should be watered once again and the growth process repeated as above. Propagate by dividing the bulbs or by removing the small bulblets that form at the base of the main bulb; plants may be grown from seed but will not come true to variety. Mealybugs, scales and spider mites can attack amaryllis; botrytis blight, leaf spot and virus are common diseases.

Hoya (HOY-a)
Wax vine

Genus of vining plants, two species of which are commonly grown as houseplants. The leaves are thick and fleshy or leathery; the flowers are small, waxy, five-lobed, star-shaped and bloom in clusters. Because of its vining habit, wax vine is excellent in a hanging basket.

Selected species and varieties. *H. bella,* miniature wax plant, has leaves that are dull green, oval to

HIBISCUS ROSA-SINENSIS

HIPPEASTRUM HYBRID

HOYA BELLA

HYACINTHUS ORIENTALIS

lance-shaped, and grow to 1¼ inches long. The flowers are ½ inch across, fragrant and white with a light pink to purple center. Plants at first grow upright to 1 foot high; the branches then droop to form a plant 1½ feet across. *H. carnosa,* wax plant, has succulent, oval to oblong leaves that grow to 3 inches long. The flowers are ½ inch across, fragrant and white with a red center. Mature plants grow to 3 feet across. 'Alba' has white flowers. 'Compacta' has leaves that are spaced closely together on the stems. 'Exotica' has leaves variegated in pink and yellow, with green margins. 'Krinkle Kurl', Hindu rope, has leaves that are folded lengthwise, curled and twisted. 'Latifolia' has wide leaves. 'Tricolor' has leaves that are copper and salmon-rose when young, and green with ivory margins when mature. Its flowers are pink. 'Variegata' has green leaves with white margins. The flowers of both species bloom during the summer.

Growing conditions. Wax plant and miniature wax plant should be grown in a room with average to warm temperature, average humidity and direct light. Miniature wax plant likes warmer temperatures than wax plant. Plant in a soilless medium; keep the medium evenly moist when the plant is in flower, and allow it to dry slightly between waterings at other times. Fertilize every month from spring to early fall. Plants will not flower until they are mature. Flowers are produced repeatedly on leafless spurs that grow from the main stem, which should not be pruned away. The stems can be allowed to trail or trained on a trellis or a wire hoop. Propagate by layering or stem cuttings in spring. Wax vine is pestered by mealybugs and aphids, but is generally disease-free.

—

Hyacinth see *Hyacinthus*

—

Hyacinthus (hy-a-SIN-thus)
Hyacinth

Spring-flowering bulb that can be forced into bloom indoors during the winter and early spring. The flowers are small, waxy, bell-shaped and highly fragrant, and bloom in dense, cylindrical clusters.

Selected species and varieties. *H. orientalis* has flower clusters that grow from 6 to 12 inches high and are surrounded by strap-shaped leaves. There are many cultivars, with flowers of white, pink, salmon, yellow, red or blue.

Growing conditions. Hyacinth bulbs must be subjected to cold treatment to be forced into bloom. In fall, plant bulbs in a well-drained, soilless medium, with the tip of the bulb flush with the surface of the medium. One bulb can be planted in a 4-inch pot, or several bulbs can be planted in a larger pot and placed so they almost touch. Water the medium well, and place the pots outdoors, either buried in the soil or protected in a cold frame, for three to four months. If the temperature does not drop below 40° F during this time, the bulbs should be chilled in a refrigerator. Then move the pots into a warm room where light is direct and humidity is average to high. Keep the growing medium evenly moist, and do not fertilize. Once the plants are in bloom, moving them to a cool room will extend their flowering period. Tall flower spikes may need to be staked. After the flowers have faded, the bulbs should be discarded. If you purchase hyacinths already in bloom, they should be treated as if they were your own forced plants brought into the house. Hyacinth bulbs are difficult if not impossible to propagate, and should be purchased. There are few insects or diseases that trouble hyacinths.

—

Hydrangea (hy-DRAN-jee-a)

Deciduous shrub, one species of which can be grown as a houseplant. Plants naturally bloom in spring and summer, but can be purchased in bloom or forced to bloom out of season. Plants have clusters of white, pink or blue flowers.

Selected species and varieties. *H. macrophylla,* French hydrangea, has 2- to 6-inch leaves that are shiny, textured, serrated, oval and dark green. Flowers are pink or blue and bloom in dense, rounded clusters. Indoors, hydrangeas grow 1½ to 2 feet tall.

Growing conditions. Place hydrangea in a room where temperature is average, humidity is average to high and light is direct. The medium should be soilless and evenly moist at all times. Purchased plants do not need to be fertilized. After the flowers have faded, plants may be moved into the garden. New plants can be propagated by cuttings. If you wish to force your own hydrangeas into bloom, plants should be potted in fall and placed outdoors in a dark cold frame for six weeks to induce flower buds before being moved indoors. Temperature must drop below 40° F for flower buds to form. Tall plants may need to be staked. The flower color of hydrangea can be changed by manipulating the pH. Blue flowers require an acidic medium; pink flowers require an alkaline medium. Hydrangea is susceptible to attack from aphids, spider mites, root knot nematodes, mildew, botrytis blight and leaf spot.

—

Impatiens (im-PAY-shens)

Perennial that can be grown as a houseplant. Plants have thick, succulent stems, oblong leaves, and single or double spurred flowers.

Selected species and varieties. *I. wallerana,* impatiens, busy Lizzie, has 6- to 18-inch stems when grown indoors, and is often grown in a hanging basket. There are a large number of varieties, which have 1- to 2-inch flowers of white, pink, orange, red, salmon, coral or violet. Some have solid-colored flowers; others are two-toned. The leaves are light to medium green and 1 to 2 inches long. Plants bloom most abundantly from spring through fall, but may flower all year.

Growing conditions. Place impatiens where temperature is average, light is direct to bright and humidity is average to high. Grow the plants in a rich, well-drained, soilless medium, and keep the medium evenly moist while the plants are flowering. Allow the medium to dry out slightly between waterings in fall and winter. Fertilize monthly from spring through fall. Pinch back growing tips regularly to

HYDRANGEA MACROPHYLLA

IMPATIENS WALLERANA

IPOMOEA PURPUREA

IRIS RETICULATA

keep the plants compact. If plants start to deteriorate, they should be discarded. New plants can be grown from stem cuttings or from seed. Impatiens can be pestered by aphids, whiteflies and spider mites, and may develop leaf spot, wilt or root rot.

—

Ipomoea (ip-o-MEE-a)
Morning glory

Genus of annual and perennial vining plants, one species of which can be grown as a houseplant. The plants have thin stems, oval to heart-shaped leaves and showy tubular flowers. They can be grown on a trellis or in a hanging basket.

Selected species and varieties. *I. purpurea* has stems that grow 3 to 4 feet long when grown indoors. The leaves are 2 to 3 inches long and heart-shaped. The flowers are trumpet-shaped, 2 to 3 inches across, and may be single or double. Bloom color is blue, purple, pink, red or white. Some flowers are solid-colored; others are striped or two-toned. Flowers last for only one day. 'Heavenly Blue Improved' has intense blue flowers with lighter blue centers. Plants can be grown to flower at any time of year.

Growing conditions. Grow morning glory in a soilless medium in a warm room where light is direct and humidity is average to high. The medium should be kept barely moist at all times. Fertilize monthly while the plant is flowering. A trellis or other support is required if the plant is not grown in a hanging basket. After the plant has flowered, it will not perform well, and should be discarded. Plants are grown from seed and will bloom in about six months. Morning glory may be attacked by aphids, mealybugs, scale, whiteflies, leaf spot or root rot.

—

Iris (I-ris)

Genus of spring-flowering bulbous and rhizomatous plants, some of which can be forced to bloom as houseplants in winter. The leaves are long, narrow and pointed. The flowers consist of three outer, drooping segments called falls and three inner, upright segments called standards.

Selected species and varieties. *I. danfordiae,* Danford iris, is a bulb that produces plants that grow 4 inches high. The flowers are bright golden yellow and appear before the leaves. *I. reticulata,* netted iris, is a bulb covered with a meshlike net. The flowers are 2 to 4 inches high, fragrant, blue, violet or purple, and flecked with yellow. The foliage emerges after the bulbs have flowered.

Growing conditions. Iris can be purchased in bloom, or you can force your own bulbs to flower. To do so, pot the bulbs in fall in a soilless medium with coarse sand added, setting the bulbs 2 inches deep and almost touching one another. Water well, and place the pots outdoors, either buried in the soil or protected in a cold frame, for six weeks to two months. If the temperature does not drop below 45° F during this time, place the bulbs in a refrigerator. Then set the pots in a cool room where light is direct and humidity is average to high. Keep the growing medium barely moist. Fertilizing is not necessary. After the flowers have faded, discard the bulbs. Bulbs may then be moved into the outdoor garden but cannot be reforced indoors. Bulbs are difficult if not impossible to propagate, and should be purchased. Iris may be attacked by aphids, spider mites and root knot nematodes, and by rot and virus diseases.

Ivy geranium see *Pelargonium*

Ixora (ik-SOR-a)

Tropical shrub that can be grown as a houseplant. The flowers are red, yellow, orange, pink or white; tubular; four- or five-lobed; and bloom in tight clusters.

Selected species and varieties. *I. coccinea,* flame-of-the-woods, grows 2 to 3 feet tall in the house. The leaves are shiny, leathery, oblong and 3 to 4 inches long. Foliage is bronze as it first develops, later changing to dark green. The flowers are bright scarlet, four-lobed and bloom in 4- to 6-inch rounded clusters. 'Fraseri' has salmon-red flowers. Flowers bloom most abundantly in late spring and summer, but may appear throughout the year.

Growing conditions. Place flame-of-the-woods in a room with warm temperature, high humidity and direct light. Grow in average, soilless potting medium and keep it evenly moist when the plant is growing and flowering. At other times, allow the medium to dry out slightly between waterings. Fertilize twice monthly during spring and summer, and monthly in fall and winter. After the plant flowers, it can be pruned to keep it compact. Increase plants by stem cuttings or from seed. Aphids, mealybugs and scales may attack flame-of-the-woods; root rot is a potential disease.

Jasmine see *Jasminum*

Jasminum (JAS-mi-num)
Jasmine

Vining tropical plant, with primarily divided leaves and clusters of tubular, star-shaped flowers, that can be grown indoors. Most species have fragrant flowers that are used in making perfume.

Selected species and varieties. *J. grandiflorum,* Catalonian jasmine, has five to seven oval, ¾-inch leaflets per leaf and white, very fragrant, ¾-inch double flowers in spring and summer. *J. nitidum,* angel-wing jasmine, is a semivining plant that has 3-inch, lance-shaped leaves. The flower buds are reddish and open into white, very fragrant, ¾-inch flowers. Plants tend to be ever-blooming. *J. officinale,* poet's jasmine, has five to seven, 2½-inch, oval leaflets and white, very fragrant, 1-inch flowers in summer and fall. 'Aureo-variegatum' has variegated leaves. *J. polyanthum,* winter jasmine,

IXORA COCCINEA

JASMINUM NITIDUM

JUSTICIA BRANDEGEANA

JUSTICIA CARNEA

has seven leathery, lance-shaped, 3-inch leaflets per leaf. The flower buds are pink, and open into white, fragrant, ¾-inch, star-shaped flowers in winter and spring. All of the species can be kept at 3 to 5 feet in height indoors by pruning.

Growing conditions. The jasmines discussed here prefer average temperature, direct light and average to high humidity. Grow them in well-drained, soilless medium and keep the medium evenly moist during spring and summer. In fall and winter, allow the medium to dry slightly between waterings. Fertilize monthly during spring and summer. After the plant has bloomed, prune it back to 6 inches high. Provide plants with a trellis, a wire hoop or another support. Plants benefit from being placed outdoors in the summer. Propagate from stem cuttings taken in summer. Mealybugs, scales and whiteflies may attack; leaf spot, root rot and virus diseases may also cause problems.

▬

Jerusalem cherry see *Solanum*

▬

Justicia (jus-TIS-ee-a)
Water willow

Tropical shrub, two species of which are commonly grown as houseplants. The leaves are lance-shaped to oval; the flowers are tubular, two-lipped, surrounded by bracts, and bloom in spikes or panicles. Plants are sometimes listed as *Jacobinia* or *Beloperone*.

Selected species and varieties. *J. brandegeana*, shrimp plant, has weak stems and is often grown in a hanging basket. The leaves are oval, soft, hairy and 3 inches long. The flowers bloom in drooping, 6-inch spikes at the ends of the stems. The flowers are white; the lower lip is spotted in red and overlapped by heart-shaped, pink, golden bronze or yellow-green bracts that look like the shells of a shrimp. 'Yellow Queen' has buttery yellow bracts. Plants bloom year round. *J. carnea*, Brazilian plume flower, has oval to oblong 4- to 8-inch leaves with prominent veins. The flowers are rose-pink to purple and surrounded by white to pink bracts, and bloom throughout the year in dense, 3- to 6-inch spikes at the ends of the stems. Plants are sometimes grown in hanging baskets. Both species are most attractive if kept pruned to 1 to 2 feet in width.

Growing conditions. Grow shrimp plant and plume flower in a warm room with bright light and high humidity. The growing medium should be rich, soilless and evenly moist. If a plant ceases to flower in winter, allow the soil to dry slightly between waterings. Fertilize every two weeks in spring and summer. In spring, cut the plant back by half, and occasionally pinch out growing tips to keep the plant compact. Propagate from stem cuttings or from seed. Shrimp plant and Brazilian plume flower can be attacked by scales and are not generally susceptible to diseases.

▬

Kaffir lily see *Clivia*

Kalanchoe (kal-an-KO-ee)

Genus of succulent plants, several species of which can be grown as houseplants. Some species are grown for their unusual leaves; others for their clusters of bright flowers.

Selected species and varieties. *K. blossfeldiana* grows 6 to 12 inches high. The leaves are oval, waxy, thick, 1 to 3 inches long and dark green edged with red lobes. The flowers are ¼ to ½ inch long, four-petaled, red, orange or yellow, and bloom in dense, rounded clusters at the tops of the plants. Flowers naturally bloom in late winter and spring, but can be forced into bloom at other times of year.

Growing conditions. Place kalanchoe in a room with average temperature, average humidity and bright to direct light. To intensify their flower color and extend the blooming period, place plants in a cool room after the flower buds have formed. Grow in well-drained, soilless medium and allow it to dry slightly between waterings. When watering, do not allow water to touch the leaves, which may cause spotting and disease. Fertilize every two weeks when the plants are growing; do not fertilize when they are in flower. To force kalanchoe to bloom in summer, fall and early winter, place it in a totally dark place for 14 hours a night for six weeks. Propagate new plants from stem or leaf cuttings or from seed. Aphids and spider mites may attack; mildew and root and crown rot are potential diseases.

KALANCHOE BLOSSFELDIANA

—

Kumquat see *Citrus*

Lace flower vine see *Episcia*

Lady's-eardrops see *Fuchsia*

Lady slipper orchid see *Paphiopedilum*

—

Lantana (lan-TAY-na)
Shrub verbena

Tropical, woody perennial or shrub that has small, tubular flowers that bloom in 1- to 2-inch rounded clusters.

Selected species and varieties. *L. camara*, yellow sage, grows best if kept pruned to 1 to 2 feet tall. The leaves are dark green, oval, toothed and rough-textured. The branches are hairy and sometimes prickly. The flowers are fragrant, pink or yellow aging to orange and red, and bloom from early spring through summer. Very often, all three colors are present on the same plant. *L. montevidensis*, trailing lantana, has vining, hairy stems that grow up to 3 feet long. The leaves are oval, rough, aromatic and toothed. The flowers are pink or lilac. Because of its growth habit, trailing lantana can be grown in a hanging basket or trained as a standard. Flowers appear on and off all year, but most abundantly in summer.

Growing conditions. Lantana likes a wide range of temperatures, and needs direct light and average humidity. Grow in soilless, well-drained medium. Keep the medium evenly moist when the plant is growing; at other times, allow it to dry slightly between waterings. Fertilize twice monthly when

LANTANA CAMARA

LILIUM LONGIFLORUM

plants are growing or flowering, and monthly at other times. After the plants have flowered, they should be pruned back by half. Pinch growing tips to encourage compact growth. Propagate from stem cuttings or from seed. Be on the lookout for white-flies, mealybugs, scales, spider and cyclamen mites, leaf spot, root rot and wilt.

Leadwort see *Plumbago*

Lemon see *Citrus*

Lilium (LIL-ee-um)
Lily

Summer-flowering bulb that can be forced for spring bloom and grown as a houseplant. Plants have erect stems, narrow and pointed leaves, and funnel-shaped flowers. Depending on species and variety, the flowers may grow upright, droop or extend outward from the stem.

Selected species and varieties. *L. longiflorum,* Easter lily, grows 3 to 5 feet tall and has dark green 5- to 7-inch leaves. The flowers are pure white, outward-facing, fragrant and 8 inches long. 'Ace' and 'Nellie White' are widely grown because of their compact habit. There are numerous other lily species and hybrids, including the American, Asiatic, Aurelian, Candidum, Mid-Century and Oriental hybrids. Many have fragrant flowers; some have reflexed petals. Colors cover the range from white to yellow, pink, red, orange, gold and lavender. Some are solid-colored; others are two-toned, striped, spotted or have throats of contrasting colors.

Growing conditions. Lilies can be purchased already in bud or bloom, or you can force your own bulbs into flower. To force your own bulbs, pot them in fall in well-drained, soilless medium, with the tip of the bulb 2 inches below the top of the medium. Water well and place the pots outdoors, buried in the ground or protected in a cold frame, for six weeks. If the temperature does not drop below 45° F during this time, place bulbs in the refrigerator. Move the pots into a room with cool to average temperature, direct light and average humidity. Keep the growing medium evenly moist and fertilize weekly with quarter-strength liquid fertilizer, beginning when the shoots first appear and ending when the flowers open. Plants will bloom in about four months. Purchased plants are grown under the same conditions. After the plants have flowered they should be discarded. The stamens of lilies can be cut off to prevent the pollen from falling on and staining furniture. Bulbs will produce small bulblets that can be removed and used to grow new plants, but greater success is achieved by purchasing new bulbs or plants every year. Lilies may also be propagated from seed, but it is a slow process, taking two to four years. Attacking insects include aphids, mealybugs and scales; diseases include leaf spot, botrytis blight and virus.

Lily see *Lilium*

Lily-of-the-Nile see *Agapanthus*

Lily-of-the-valley see *Convallaria*

Lipstick plant see *Aeschynanthus*

Living-vase see *Aechmea*

Lucky clover see *Oxalis*

—

Lycoris (ly-KOR-is)

Bulb commonly grown as a tub plant outdoors or as a houseplant. The leaves are strap-shaped and develop after the flowers appear. The flowers are fragrant and tubular and have flaring petals. The stamens are long, prominent and showy. Flowers bloom in clusters at the tops of solid, leafless stems in fall.

Selected species and varieties. *L. africana,* golden spider lily, has leaves that are 12 inches long and ¾ inch wide. The flowers are 3 inches long and golden yellow, and bloom on 15-inch stems. The petals have wavy margins and are recurved. *L. radiata,* formerly sold as *Nerine sarniensis,* red spider lily, grows 16 to 18 inches high. The leaves are 12 inches long and ½ inch wide. The flowers are pink to deep red and 1½ inches long, with narrow, crisped, recurved petals. 'Alba' has white flowers. *L. squamigera,* magic lily, resurrection lily, grows 2 feet tall. The leaves are 12 inches long and 1 inch wide. The flowers are 3 inches long, rose-lilac or purple with a yellow base, and fragrant.

Growing conditions. In late summer, pot bulbs in a well-drained, soilless medium. Place pots in a room where temperature is average, light is direct and humidity is average. Allow the medium to dry out slightly between waterings. The flowers appear quickly, and are followed by the foliage. Remove the flowers after they fade, and continue watering the plant until the foliage turns brown in the spring. Let the pots dry out, and store them over the summer in a warm place. In late summer, start watering and let the process repeat itself. Plants can be propagated by removing and growing the small bulblets that form at the base of the mother bulb. Mealybugs and scales may infest plants, and leaf spot is a potential disease.

—

Madagascar jasmine see *Stephanotis*

Magic flower see *Achimenes*

Magic lily see *Lycoris*

Mandarin orange see *Citrus*

—

Mandevilla (man-da-VIL-a)

Genus of tropical, vining shrubs, one species of which is grown as a houseplant. The leaves have small glands at their bases or along their midribs. The flowers open only during the day. They are funnel-shaped and bloom in clusters. When stems or leaves are bruised, a milky sap is emitted. *Mandevilla* was formerly designated as the *Dipladenia* genus.

Selected species and varieties. *M. × amabilis* has oval to oblong 2-inch leaves that cover twining branches. The flowers are single, large and showy, pale pink when they open, darkening to deep rose.

LYCORIS SQUAMIGERA

MANDEVILLA × AMABILIS 'ALICE DU PONT'

MUSCARI ARMENIACUM

'Alice du Pont' has 3- to 8-inch, dark green, shiny, textured leaves and 2½- to 4-inch pale pink flowers that have a deep rose throat and age to dark rose. Plants bloom in spring and summer.

Growing conditions. Grow mandevilla where temperature is high, humidity is high and light is bright. Grow in all-purpose, soilless medium, and allow it to dry slightly between waterings. Fertilize every two weeks when the plant is growing or flowering. After the plant has flowered, cut it back to control its size, which is best kept at about 3 feet. Provide a wire hoop or other support. Propagate by stem cuttings. Plants are generally resistant to diseases, but thrips and mealybugs occasionally attack.

Martha Washington geranium
see *Pelargonium*

Morning glory see *Ipomoea*

Mother of thousands see *Saxifraga*

Moth orchid see *Phalaenopsis*

Muscari (mus-KAR-ee)
Grape hyacinth

Spring-flowering bulb that can be grown indoors and forced to bloom in winter. The leaves are grasslike and blue-green. The flowers are fragrant, bell-shaped and bloom in cone-shaped spikes.

Selected species and varieties. *M. armeniacum* grows 9 inches tall. The flowers are oblong, ⅜ inch long and blue to deep violet with white edges. 'Blue Spike' has branched, dense flower clusters. *M. azureum* grows to 8 inches high. The flowers are blue and 3/16 inch long. The bottoms of the flowers do not curve inward as they do in other species. 'Album' has white flowers. 'Amphibolis' has light blue flowers. *M. botryoides* grows to 12 inches tall. Its flowers are round, ⅛ inch long and blue with white edges. 'Album' has white flowers. 'Caeruleum' has bright blue flowers. 'Carneum' has pale pink flowers.

Growing conditions. Grape hyacinth may be purchased in bloom, or you can force your own bulbs if you chill them first. Pot the bulbs in the fall in well-drained, soilless medium, with the tips of the bulbs just above the top of the medium. Store them outdoors in a dark cold frame for eight to 12 weeks before moving them inside. If outdoor temperature does not drop to 40° F, the bulbs must be chilled in the refrigerator. Place pots in a room where temperature is cool, humidity is average and light is direct. Keep the medium evenly moist. After the flowers have faded, discard the bulbs. The small bulblets that form at the base of the mother bulb can be removed and potted to start new plants. Grape hyacinth is not generally susceptible to insects or diseases.

Narcissus (nar-SIS-us)
Daffodil

Spring-flowering bulb that can be forced into bloom for use as a houseplant in winter and early spring.

The foliage is narrow, flat and strap-shaped, growing from the base of the plant. Flowers bloom on thick, leafless stems. The center of the flower is trumpet- or cup-shaped, and is surrounded by six petals.

Selected species and varieties. Two types of daffodils are commonly forced for use as houseplants. Trumpet daffodils have tubular centers that are longer than the petals, and may be solid yellow, solid white, or have white trumpets and yellow petals. The Tazetta daffodils have clusters of small, fragrant, yellow or white flowers with cup-shaped centers. 'Paper White' is the variety most used for forcing.

Growing conditions. You can purchase plants in bloom or force bulbs into bloom yourself. To force bulbs into bloom, plant them in well-drained soilless medium in fall, with the tip of the bulb 1 inch below the surface of the medium. Tazetta daffodils can be forced using pebbles as the medium. Water well, and place the pots outdoors, either buried in the ground or protected in a cold frame, for 10 to 12 weeks. If the outdoor temperature does not drop to 35° F, bulbs must be placed in the refrigerator. Move the pots into a room with average temperature, direct light and average humidity. Bulbs will bloom in 10 days to three weeks. During this time, and until flowers fade, keep the growing medium evenly moist. Fertilizing is not necessary. Tall plants may need to be staked. After the flowers fade, the bulbs should be discarded. New bulbs can be propagated by removing and planting the small bulblets that form around the base of the main bulb, but greater success is achieved by buying new plants or bulbs each year. Daffodils can be attacked by spider mites and by bulb rot and root rot.

Nasturtium see *Tropaeolum*

Natal plum see *Carissa*

Nerine (ne-RY-nee)

Autumn-flowering bulb that can be grown as a houseplant. The leaves are strap-shaped, grow from the base of the plant and appear after the flowers. The flowers are funnel-shaped and bloom in clusters on top of leafless stems.

Selected species and varieties. *N. sarniensis,* Guernsey lily, has 12-inch leaves. The flowers are crimson, 1½ inches long, and have crisped petals and bright red, long, straight stamens. They bloom on 18-inch stems. 'Maxima' has slightly larger flowers.

Growing conditions. Grow Guernsey lily in a cool temperature, direct light and average to high humidity. Plant in a rich, soilless medium, with half the bulb extending above the surface of the medium. Water well, and then allow the medium to dry slightly between waterings. Fertilize every two weeks from the time growth starts until early spring, when the foliage turns yellow and dies down. Store the pots in a dark, 50° F area until midsummer, when the plants should be watered and brought back into the

NARCISSUS 'PAPER WHITE'

NERINE SARNIENSIS

NERIUM OLEANDER

NIDULARIUM INNOCENTII

house, and the process repeated. Propagate by dividing the bulbs or removing and planting the small bulblets that form around the base of the main bulb. Mealybugs, scales, thrips and spider mites can attack; botrytis blight, leaf spot and virus are common diseases.

—

Nerium (NEER-ee-um)
Oleander

Genus of tropical and subtropical trees and shrubs, one species of which can be grown as a houseplant. The branches grow upright and are covered with whorls of lance-shaped, narrow leaves. The flowers are tubular and bloom in clusters at the ends of the branches.

Selected species and varieties. *N. oleander,* rosebay, grows up to 4 feet high indoors, but can be kept lower by pruning. The leaves are very narrow, dark, dull green, leathery and up to 10 inches long. The flowers have five petals and may be white, yellow, pink, rose or reddish purple. Some are fragrant; all bloom in spring and summer. 'Album' has white flowers. 'Atropurpureum' has carmine flowers. 'Roseum' has rose-pink flowers. 'Variegata' has rose-red flowers and leaves that are striped and edged in yellow or creamy white. All parts of the oleander plant are toxic.

Growing conditions. Grow oleander where temperature is average, light is direct and humidity is average to high. In winter, plants benefit from cool temperature. Plant in a soilless growing medium, and keep the medium evenly moist at all times. Fertilize every two weeks while plants are growing and flowering. Prune back plants after they have flowered, and pinch growing tips to keep the plants compact. Propagate from rooting tip cuttings. Aphids and mealybugs, and especially scales, are insects that attack oleander; leaf spot is the most serious disease.

—

Nidularium (nee-dew-LAR-ee-um)

A bromeliad having dense, spreading, prickly-margined leaves that form a basal rosette that collects water. When the plant is about to flower, the base of the leaves near the center of the rosette turns color, usually rose-red to dark red. The flowers are surrounded by colorful bracts and grow in small clusters in the center of the plant. They may bloom at any time of year.

Selected species and varieties. *N. fulgens,* blushing bromeliad, has leaves that grow up to 12 inches long. They are pea green spotted with dark green and have ¼-inch spines. The flowers are white or blue, surrounded by bright scarlet bracts tipped in green and bloom in dense clusters. *N. innocentii* has 12-inch, strap-shaped leaves that have short spines; the leaves turn metallic purple at the base when the plant is about to flower. The flowers are white, 2½ inches long and are surrounded by red bracts that are sometimes tipped in green.

Growing conditions. Nidularium is grown where temperature is warm, light is bright and humidity is low. Grow plants in a rich, coarse, soilless medium, and keep it evenly moist at all times. Make sure that there is always water in the cup at the base of the plant. Fertilize every month with quarter-strength liquid fertilizer. Propagate by removing and planting the offshoots that grow at the base of the plant after it flowers, by division or from seed. Nidularium is usually not bothered by insects or diseases, but scales and crown rot may occasionally attack.

—

Odontoglossum (o-don-toh-GLOS-um)

Large genus of orchids, some of which can be grown as houseplants. Plants have one or two folded leaves and showy flowers that bloom in sprays. Individual flowers have clawed lips and five spreading petals.

Selected species and varieties. *O. grande,* tiger orchid, has 6-inch flowers of yellow marked in reddish brown. It blooms most abundantly from late fall to early spring. Plants grow up to 3 feet tall. There are many hybrids, which have 3- to 4-inch flowers on 2- to 3-foot stems. Many are white or yellow and marked in a darker color.

Growing conditions. Odontoglossums prefer cool temperature and high humidity. Place them in bright light in summer and in direct light the rest of the year. Pot in a growing mix designed for orchids, one to which fir or redwood bark or osmunda fiber has been added, and keep it evenly moist. Fertilize monthly; use a complete fertilizer. Tall plants need to be staked. Propagate by dividing the rhizome, making sure that each division has three pseudobulbs, which are food- and water-storing tissue. Odontoglossums may be damaged by scales, mealybugs, spider mites or virus diseases.

—

Oleander see *Nerium*

—

Oncidium (on-SID-ee-um)
Dancing-lady orchid

Genus of orchid with flat, fleshy leaves and small, showy flowers that appear in large, arching sprays.

Selected species and varieties. There are many hybrids that are easy to grow indoors. Plants vary in height from only a few inches to several feet, have leaves that may be thin or thick and succulent, and produce flowering sprays from 1 to 3 feet long. Flower color varies, and many flowers are spotted in darker colors. Blooming occurs at various times throughout the year, depending on the species.

Growing conditions. Dancing-lady orchids with thin leaves should be grown in bright light; those with succulent leaves prefer direct light. Humidity must be high; temperature should be average. Grow in a soilless medium that contains fir or redwood bark or osmunda fiber. Dwarf varieties can be grown on slabs of tree fern. When the plant is growing and flowering, keep the medium evenly moist and fertilize twice monthly; allow the medium to dry slightly between waterings at other times and do not fertilize. Taller varieties may need support. Propagate by

ODONTOGLOSSUM GRANDE

ONCIDIUM HYBRID

117

ORNITHOGALUM ARABICUM

OXALIS DEPPEI

dividing the rhizome, making sure that each division has three pseudobulbs, which are food- and water-storing tissue. Scales, mealybugs, spider mites and virus diseases may attack.

Orange see *Citrus*

Orchid cactus see *Epiphyllum*

Ornithogalum (or-ni-THOG-a-lum)

Spring-blooming bulb that can be grown as a houseplant for bloom in winter and spring. The leaves are narrow and grasslike, and grow from the base of the plant. The flowers are fragrant, have six petals, are star-shaped and bloom in clusters.

Selected species and varieties. *O. arabicum,* star-of-Bethlehem, has white, 1- to 2-inch flowers that bloom in clusters of six to 12. Plants grow 12 to 24 inches high. *O. caudatum,* sea onion, grows 18 to 36 inches high. The flowers are white with a green midvein on the petals, 1 inch across and bloom in clusters of up to 100 flowers. *O. thyrsoides,* wonder flower, grows 6 to 18 inches high and has cream-colored to white 1- to 2-inch flowers that are brown at the base. The flowers of this species are very long lasting and are often used as cut flowers. *O. umbellatum,* star-of-Bethlehem, grows 8 to 12 inches high. The leaves have a white midvein. The flowers are white and 1 inch across.

Growing conditions. Grow ornithogalum in a cool room where light is direct and humidity is average. Plant bulbs in a soilless medium, and let the medium dry slightly between waterings. Fertilize monthly when the plant is growing or flowering. Unlike many other bulbs, ornithogalum does not require a chilling period. After the flowers have faded, water until the foliage turns brown. Then let the medium dry out and place potted bulbs in a storage area over the summer and fall. In early winter, bring the pots into the house, start watering and repeat the process. Propagate during the dormant period by removing and planting the small bulblets that form at the base of the main bulb. Insects do not attack; leaf spot is a potential disease.

Oxalis (OK-sal-is)

Genus of annuals and perennials, some of which can be grown as houseplants. Plants grow from bulbs, tubers or rhizomes, and have three-part, cloverlike leaves at the base. Flowers are available in all colors except blue; they are single and five-petaled and bloom indoors from fall through spring. Blooms open only on sunny days and close up at night.

Selected species and varieties. *O. deppei,* four-leaf clover, lucky clover, grows to 1¼ feet tall, and has four oval leaflets that are 1½ inches long and red flowers. *O. rosea* is a multibranched plant that grows to 18 inches high. Each leaflet is ½ inch long. The flowers are rose and have darker veins and white throats. They bloom in loose, several-flowered clusters. *O. rubra* grows 12 inches high and has three ¾-inch-long leaflets that are coppery green and hairy. The flowers are pink, rose or lilac with darker red veins. 'Alba' has white flowers. The stems are weak and plants are often grown in hanging baskets.

Growing conditions. Grow oxalis in a cool to average room where light is direct and humidity is average. Plant in a well-drained, soilless medium that is allowed to dry out slightly between waterings. Fertilize monthly during the growing and flowering period. After the plant has flowered, the foliage turns brown and dies back. Store the plants in their pots until fall, when they should be returned to the house and the process repeated. Plants can be propagated by division or from seed.

Pachystachys (pak-i-STAK-is)

Genus of tropical shrubs, one species of which is commonly grown as a houseplant. The leaves are large; the flowers bloom in a spike at the top of the plant in the summer.

Selected species and varieties. *P. lutea* grows about 12 inches high indoors. The leaves are oval, 5 inches long and dark green with depressed veins. The flower spike is 4 inches long; the flowers are white, 2 inches long and burst open from golden yellow, heart-shaped, 1-inch bracts.

Growing conditions. Grow pachystachys in a warm room with bright light and high humidity. The growing medium should be soilless and well drained, and watered so it is evenly moist at all times. Fertilize monthly during the growing and flowering periods. Propagate from stem cuttings in spring. Pachystachys is generally free of insects and diseases.

Painted feather see *Vriesea*
Painted lady see *Echeveria*
Panama orange see *Citrus*

Paphiopedilum (pa-fee-o-PEE-di-lum)
Lady slipper orchid

Genus of orchids having leathery leaves that are either solid green or mottled. In the lower center of the flower is a large pouch-shaped lip that is surrounded by one large and two slim, waxy petals. Plants grow from 4 to 12 inches high and bloom most abundantly in fall through spring. The types with spotted or marbled leaves are among the easiest orchids to grow in the house.

Selected species and varieties. There are a large number of species and hybrids of lady slipper orchid, which have blooms that are 3 to 5 inches across. Flower color may be white, brown, purple, green, pink or yellow.

Growing conditions. Grow lady slipper orchid in bright light, average to warm temperature and high humidity. If light is too high, the leaves turn yellow and flowering decreases. Grow in a soilless, well-drained medium to which additional sphagnum peat moss or osmunda fiber has been added, and keep it

PACHYSTACHYS LUTEA

PAPHIOPEDILUM HYBRID

PASSIFLORA CAERULEA

PELARGONIUM PELTATUM

evenly moist at all times. Fertilize monthly. Propagate by division or from seed. Lady slipper orchids may be attacked by mealybugs, spider mites, scales or virus diseases.

Passiflora (pas-i-FLOR-a)
Passionflower

Vigorous tropical vine, several species of which can be grown as houseplants. The leaves have three or more deep lobes. The flowers have 10 outer petals; an odd-shaped, tubular structure protrudes from the center of the flower and is surrounded by several rings of thin, fringed filaments. Although each flower lasts only one day, plants bloom over a long period from spring through late summer. Plants grow 6 to 10 feet high indoors.

Selected species and varieties. *P.* × *alato-caerulea* has three-lobed leaves and fragrant pink petals with a fringed crown of purple, blue and white. *P. caerulea,* blue passionflower, has leaves that are gray-green and 4 to 5 inches across with five to nine deep lobes. The outer petals are white or off-white; the filaments are blue, purple or white. Flowers are fragrant. 'Grandiflora' has 5- to 6-inch flowers. 'Constance Elliot' has white flowers. *P. coccinea,* red passionflower, has 3- to 6-inch oval, coarse leaves and flowers with scarlet petals and filaments of deep purple and pink. *P. edulis,* purple granadilla, has three-lobed, 4- to 6-inch leaves with wavy edges. The flowers are white and purple. *P. trifasciata* has leaves with three slight lobes; they are satiny olive green to deep bronze, with three broad, pink to silvery zones across the purple veins, and are purple on the undersides. The flowers are fragrant and yellow.

Growing conditions. Passionflower prefers an average to warm temperature, direct light and average humidity. Grow it in well-drained, soilless medium and keep it constantly moist during the growing and flowering period. At other times, allow the medium to dry slightly between waterings. Fertilize twice a month during the growing and flowering period. After the vine has flowered, cut it back to 6 inches high. Passionflower must be trained on a trellis, wire loop or other support. Propagate by stem cuttings or from seed. Mealybugs, scales and root knot nematodes are the main insects that attack passionflower; it is susceptible to leaf spot.

Passionflower see *Passiflora*
Peace lily see *Spathiphyllum*

Pelargonium (pel-ar-GO-nee-um)
Geranium

Genus of annuals and perennials grown for their showy flowers or for their foliage, depending on the species. Flowers appear most abundantly from spring through fall, and off and on during the winter if the plants have enough light.

Selected species and varieties. *P.* × *domesticum,* Martha Washington geranium, grows 1 to 2 feet high. The leaves are 2 to 4 inches across, toothed, and lobed or deeply divided. The flowers are white, red, pink or purple, and have blotches of contrasting colors on the petals. *P.* × *hortorum,* zonal geranium, garden geranium, grows 6 to 24 inches high indoors. The leaves are round to heart-shaped, 3 to 5 inches across and have scalloped edges. Some varieties have a brown or black band around the leaf. The flowers bloom in dense, rounded clusters on long stems and are white, pink, red, salmon, coral, rose or violet. *P. peltatum,* ivy geranium, has stems that grow up to 3 feet long and is best grown in a hanging basket. Leaves are 2 to 3 inches across and lobed; flowers bloom in loose, airy clusters and are white, pink, red or lavender.

Growing conditions. Geraniums should be grown in a cool to average room with direct light and average humidity. Martha Washington geraniums need cooler temperatures than other geraniums. Geraniums grow well under fluorescent lights, especially in winter, when natural light may be insufficient for flowering. Plant in well-drained, soilless medium, and let it dry slightly between waterings. In winter, water sparingly, just enough to keep the plant from wilting. Fertilize every two weeks from early spring to midfall. Remove flowers as they fade. Pinch out growing tips to encourage branching and compact growth. Geraniums become woody after several years, and are best discarded after cuttings are taken for new plants. Some varieties may also be grown from seeds. Geraniums are susceptible to aphids, mealybugs, whiteflies, spider mites, damping-off, edema, blights, virus, and root and stem rots.

PENTAS LANCEOLATA

Pentas (PEN-tas)

Genus of perennials and small shrubs, one species of which is grown as a houseplant. The leaves are oval to lance-shaped; the flowers are small and bloom in dense clusters at the ends of the branches.

Selected species and varieties. *P. lanceolata,* star cluster, Egyptian star, is most attractive indoors if kept at 12 to 18 inches high by pruning and pinching. The leaves are bright green, hairy, 3 to 4 inches long and deeply veined. The flowers are ¾ to 1½ inches long, tubular, star-shaped and bloom in 4-inch clusters. They may be white, pink, magenta or lilac in color. Flowers appear most abundantly in winter and spring.

Growing conditions. Grow star cluster in a room that has average to warm temperature, direct light and average humidity. The medium should be soilless and well drained and kept evenly moist. Fertilize every two weeks while the plant is growing and flowering. After the flowers have faded, prune the plants back to half their former size, and use the prunings to root new plants. Pinch growing tips to keep the plants bushy and compact. Scales are the major insects that attack star cluster; it is generally resistant to disease.

Pepper see *Capsicum*
Persian violet
see *Cyclamen; Exacum*

PHALAENOPSIS HYBRID

PHALAENOPSIS HYBRID

Phalaenopsis (fal-e-NOP-sis)
Moth orchid

Genus of orchids having shiny, erect or arching, strap-shaped leaves. The flowers are flat, with five round petals and a small, three-lobed lip. Flowers bloom in arching sprays and resemble winged insects in flight.

Selected species and varieties. There are a large number of species and hybrids of moth orchid. The species orchids bloom most abundantly in winter and spring; the hybrids may bloom at any time of year. Flowers are 2 to 4 inches across. Flowers may be white, pink, yellow, violet or red, or marked in combinations of two colors.

Growing conditions. Grow moth orchid in a room with cool temperature in fall and average to warm temperature the rest of the year. Light should be bright from fall through spring and limited in summer; humidity should be high. Grow in a well-drained, soilless medium with extra fir or redwood bark or osmunda fiber. Keep the medium evenly moist at all times. Fertilize twice monthly when the plant is growing or flowering. Use a complete fertilizer. Moth orchid may be propagated from seed or by removing and planting the small plantlets that form on the flower spike. Scales, mealybugs, spider mites and virus may attack.

Pineapple see *Ananas*

Plumbago (plum-BAY-go)
Leadwort

Genus of perennials and shrubs, some of them vining. Flowers have slender tubes that open into five spreading lobes, and bloom in clusters at the ends of the branches from late winter through summer.

Selected species and varieties. *P. auriculata,* formerly designated *P. capensis,* Cape leadwort, grows to 4 feet tall and has slender, arching stems. The leaves are oblong and 2 inches long. The flowers are 1½ inches long and blue. 'Alba' has white flowers.

Growing conditions. Grow Cape leadwort in average to warm temperature, direct light and average humidity. In winter, temperature should be cool. The medium should be soilless, well drained, kept evenly moist at all times in spring, summer and fall, and allowed to dry slightly between waterings in winter. Fertilize once a month in spring and summer. Prune the plants in winter before new growth starts, and use the prunings to root new plants. Plants may also be propagated from seed or by division. Mealybugs and scales are the most common insect problems; plumbago is resistant to diseases.

Pocketbook plant see *Calceolaria*
Poinsettia see *Euphorbia*
Pomegranate see *Punica*
Pot marigold see *Calendula*

Primrose see *Primula*

PLUMBAGO AURICULATA

Primula (PRIM-u-la)
Primrose

Genus of perennials, some of which can be grown as houseplants. They grow 6 to 12 inches tall and have leaves that form at the base of the plant. The flowers are funnel-shaped, opening into flat, single, lobed flowers that bloom in rounded clusters during winter and spring.

Selected species and varieties. *P. malacoides,* fairy primrose, has light green, papery, toothed leaves that have hairy undersides. Flowers are less than 1 inch across; white, pink, rose, red or lavender; and bloom in tiers on thin stems. 'Alba' has white flowers. The King series grows 8 inches high and has lavender, red, rose or white flowers. 'Pink Ice' has fragrant, rose-pink flowers. 'Rosea' has bright rose flowers. 'Snow Cone' blooms very early, with pure white flowers. *P. obconica,* German primrose, has 10-inch, round to heart-shaped, rough, hairy leaves that cause a skin rash in some people. Flowers are fragrant; 1 to 2 inches across; and white, pink, lavender or red with a green eye. 'Gigantea' is larger than the species. 'Grandiflora' has large flowers. *P. × polyantha,* polyantha primrose, has oval to oblong, 6-inch leaves. The flowers are fragrant; 1 to 2 inches wide; and white, yellow, pink, red, lavender, purple, orange or maroon, often with a white eye. *P. sinensis,* Chinese primrose, grows 12 inches high and has 5-inch heart-shaped, lobed, hairy leaves. Flowers are 1½ inches across and are available in all colors. 'Filicifolia' has crisped leaves. 'Fimbriata' has fringed flowers. 'Stellata', star primrose, has star-shaped double flowers. *P. vulgaris,* sometimes designated *P. acaulis,* English primrose, grows 6 inches high and has 10-inch, wrinkled, oblong leaves. The flowers are yellow, purple, blue, pink, rose, red, white or apricot. There are many named varieties, including the Crown, Ducat, Festive, Lovely, Pageant, Saga and Spectrum series. These are the primroses most often sold by florists.

Growing conditions. Primroses like a place indoors where temperature is cool, light is bright and humidity is high. Plant in a rich, soilless medium and keep it evenly moist. Fertilize every two weeks in spring, summer and fall. Plants are usually discarded after the flowers have faded, but they can be moved into a shaded outdoor garden. Primroses are increased by division or grown from seed sown in spring or fall, in which case they will grow into flowering plants in seven to 12 months. Spider mites, whiteflies, mealybugs and aphids are the major insect pests; plants are susceptible to damping-off and crown rot.

PRIMULA × POLYANTHA

Punica (PEW-ni-ka)
Pomegranate

Tropical or subtropical fruit tree that can be grown indoors for decoration and edible fruit.

Selected species and varieties. *P. granatum* grows to 10 feet indoors. The leaves are oblong, 3

PUNICA GRANATUM 'NANA'

RHODODENDRON SIMSII

inches long and glossy green. The flowers have a purple, 1½-inch tube that opens into five to eight crinkled, orange-red lobes. Plants bloom most abundantly in spring and summer. The flowers are followed by 2½- to 5-inch, yellow, orange, red or purple edible fruit. The variety 'Nana' is grown indoors more often than the species, because it grows only 15 to 18 inches high. It has narrow, bright glossy green ¾- to 1½-inch leaves. The flowers are bright red to orange-red and 2 inches long.

Growing conditions. Set pomegranate in a spot where temperature is average, light is direct and humidity is average. In winter, place the plant in a cool room. Grow plants in a well-drained, extra-rich, soilless medium, and keep it evenly moist from early spring to midfall. During late fall and winter, water only enough to keep the plant from wilting. Fertilize every two weeks during spring and summer. In early spring, prune back if needed to control size or to shape the plant. Plants start to produce fruit when they are three to four years old; fruit ripens best if it is picked and allowed to ripen off the plant. Propagate new plants by stem cuttings, by layering or from seed. Insects that bother pomegranate include aphids, mealybugs, spider mites, scales and whiteflies; diseases include root rot and various diseases that cause the fruit to rot.

—

Purple granadilla see *Passiflora*
Queen's tears see *Billbergia*
Rain lily see *Zephyranthes*
Resurrection lily see *Lycoris*
Rex begonia see *Begonia*

—

Rhododendron (ro-doh-DEN-dron)
Azalea

Genus of shrubby evergreen and deciduous spring-flowering shrubs that may be forced into bloom for use as houseplants in late winter and early spring. All azaleas are members of the *Rhododendron* genus, but not all members of the genus are azaleas. The species vary greatly in plant size and foliage. The flowers are funnel-shaped and bloom in clusters. They may be single or double, and white, pink, rose, red, lavender, purple, yellow or orange.

Selected species and varieties. *R. simsii,* Sims's azalea, Indian azalea, grows 12 inches high indoors. Leaves are dark green, leathery, 1½ to 2 inches long and oblong to oval. Flowers are 2 inches across, white, rose or red, and often spotted in darker tones. There are many *R.* hybrids that are commonly known as florist's azaleas. Most grow 8 to 24 inches high and have small, rounded, glossy leaves. 'Alaska' has single, semidouble or double white flowers that have a yellow-green blotch on the petals. 'Chimes' has semidouble red flowers. 'Dorothy Gish' has red flowers that grow in a form called hose-in-hose (one single flower set inside another single flower). 'Erie', sometimes designated 'Eri', has double pink flowers with a white edge. 'Lentengroot', sometimes designated 'Lentegroet' or 'Easter Greeting', has single red blooms. 'Red-

Wing' has hose-in-hose red flowers. 'Sweetheart Supreme' has deep pink blooms that may be hose-in-hose or semidouble.

Growing conditions. Azaleas should be placed in a room where temperature is cool, light is direct and humidity is high. The medium should be soilless, rich, slightly acidic, and well drained. Forced plants do not need fertilizing when they are in bloom. After the flowers have faded, remove them and prune the plants to shape them if necessary. The hardiness of forced azaleas varies considerably with the variety, but they may survive if planted outdoors where minimum winter temperature is between $-10°$ and $30°$ F. To force your own azaleas into bloom, grow them outdoors in pots in partial shade over the summer. Fertilize monthly. In fall, plants must have four to eight weeks of $35°$ to $50°$ F temperature to set flower buds, after which they should be moved indoors for forcing. Azaleas are propagated by stem cuttings or from seed. Attacking insects include aphids, spider and cyclamen mites, and mealybugs; diseases include botrytis blight, leaf spot, and root and stem rot. Yellow leaves may indicate iron chlorosis. Check to be sure that the pH is acidic and treat the medium with chelated iron if necessary.

—

ROSA (MINIATURE)

Rosa (RO-za)
Rose

Genus of shrubs, some of which can be grown indoors. The leaves have five to nine leaflets; the flowers are single to double, often fragrant, and any color except true blue. Plants can flower indoors all year if they receive enough light.

Selected species and varieties. Miniature roses are the roses most often grown indoors. There are hundreds of hybrids that have all the attributes of their larger cousins, except that everything is smaller—the flowers, the leaves and the stems. All miniature rose hybrids available are descendants of *R. chinensis minima.* Miniature roses grow from 4 to 18 inches high indoors. Excellent varieties are orange 'Starina' and 'Holy Toledo'; white 'Simplex' and 'Pacesetter'; yellow and pink blend 'Rainbow's End'; apricot 'Jean Kenneally'; red and white blend 'Magic Carrousel', 'Toy Clown' and 'Dreamglo'; pink 'Rosmarin' and 'Cupcake'; yellow 'Rise 'n' Shine'; and red 'Beauty Secret' and 'Black Jade'.

Growing conditions. Place miniature roses in a room where temperature is average, light is direct and humidity is high. Plants can be grown under fluorescent lights in the winter, if natural light is insufficient. The growing medium should be rich, soilless and well drained. Keep it evenly moist at all times. Fertilize every two weeks while the plant is growing or flowering. Cut back the stems after the flowers have faded to shape the plant and control its size. Spider mites are the most troublesome insects, but miniature roses can also be troubled by aphids, thrips, mildew and black spot indoors.

—

Rose see *Rosa*

Rosebay see *Nerium*

Rosemary see *Rosmarinus*

ROSMARINUS OFFICINALIS

SAINTPAULIA IONANTHA

Rosmarinus (ros-ma-RY-nus)
Rosemary

Perennial or small shrub that can be grown indoors either for decoration or as a culinary herb. Leaves are needle-shaped and aromatic. The flowers are tubular and two-lipped, and bloom in spikes during winter and early spring.

Selected species and varieties. *R. officinalis* grows 1 to 3 feet high. The leaves are ½ to 1½ inches long, dark green and shiny on the upper surfaces, and fuzzy white on the undersides. The flowers are fragrant and blue or lavender, although there are varieties with white or pink flowers. 'Albus' has white flowers. 'Prostratus' is low-growing with long stems, and may be grown in a hanging basket. 'Tuscan Blue' has rigid stems and bright blue-violet flowers.

Growing conditions. Grow rosemary where temperature is average, light is direct and humidity is average. It will benefit from being moved to a cool room in winter. Plant it in a soilless medium that is allowed to dry slightly between waterings. Fertilize every two months from midspring to midfall. Pinch growing tips to keep the plants compact. Leaves may be removed at any time and used fresh or dried in cooking. Propagate new plants from seed or from cuttings taken in spring or summer. Rosemary is resistant to insects, but is susceptible to root rot.

Saintpaulia (saint-PAUL-ee-a)
African violet

Genus of plants in the gesneriad family, one species of which is grown as a houseplant. Leaves are heart-shaped and hairy, and grow in a basal rosette. The flowers resemble violets and are flat and five-lobed.

Selected species and varieties. *S. ionantha* grows 4 to 6 inches high. Some varieties have green leaves; others have bronze or variegated leaves. There are many hybrids that have white, pink, rose, blue, purple or two-toned flowers that are 1 inch across and may be single or double. There are also varieties with ruffled or frilled petals. The hybrids flower freely and will bloom throughout the year if given enough light.

Growing conditions. African violets prefer a place where temperature is warm, light is bright and humidity is medium to high. Plant them in a rich, soilless, well-drained medium, and keep it evenly moist at all times. Be careful when watering not to drop water on the leaves or they will spot, and water only with warm water to prevent rings from developing on the leaves. When planting, ensure that the crown of the plant is above the level of the medium. Plants can be grown under fluorescent lights, especially in the winter, to ensure maximum blooming. Fertilize twice a month when the plant is growing and flowering. Leaves that touch the rim of the pot are sometimes killed by contact with the soluble salts that build up on the rim. To prevent this, line the rim with aluminum foil or wax. New plants are propagated from leaf cuttings, by division or from seed. Insects that may attack are aphids, mealybugs, thrips, root knot nematodes, and spider and cyclamen mites.

Diseases include botrytis blight, and crown and root rot. Keep the air circulating freely around the plants to reduce the chance of disease.

—

Saxifraga (saks-IF-ra-ga)

Large genus of perennials, one species of which is often grown as a houseplant. Leaves grow in basal rosettes. The flowers bloom in delicate, airy, nodding clusters in late spring and summer.

Selected species and varieties. *S. stolonifera,* strawberry geranium, mother of thousands, has round, scalloped, hairy, 3- to 4-inch leaves that are dark green with silver stripes on the upper surfaces and red on the undersides. Plants grow 6 to 9 inches tall and produce runners that grow up to 2 feet long. New plants form at the ends of the runners. Because of its long runners and the plantlets that suspend from them, strawberry geranium grows best in a hanging basket. The flowers are 1 inch across, white and bloom on thin stems.

Growing conditions. Grow strawberry geranium in moderate temperatures and humidity and in direct light. Plant it in well-drained, soilless medium. From spring through fall, keep the medium evenly moist; in winter, allow it to dry slightly between watering. Fertilize every two months during spring and summer. New plants are propagated by removing and planting the plantlets that form at the ends of the runners. Plants can also be grown by division or from seed. Insects rarely attack strawberry geranium, but it is susceptible to root rot.

—

Scarlet basket vine see *Aeschynanthus*
Scarlet plume see *Euphorbia*

—

Schlumbergera (shlum-BER-jer-a)

Member of the cactus family that is included in a group known as jungle cactus because it requires higher moisture and humidity than desert cactus does. The plant has flattened, leafless stems consisting of jointed segments that are leaf-shaped and 1½ to 2 inches long. The flowers are 3 inches long and tubular, with flaring petals that open up into a cup or funnel shape. They are drooping, and white, pink, red, lavender, purple or orange. Depending on the species, they bloom in fall or winter. Because of the plant's drooping growth habit, it can be grown in a hanging basket.

Selected species and varieties. *S. bridgesii,* Christmas cactus, has branches made up of 2-inch segments that have rounded margins. It blooms during the winter. *S. truncata,* Thanksgiving cactus, has branches made up of 2-inch segments that have toothed margins. It blooms during the fall.

Growing conditions. Place Christmas cactus in a room where light is bright and humidity is medium to high. The room should be warm from early spring to fall when the plant is growing, and cool in fall when the plant is setting flower buds. Plants are grown in a rich, soilless, well-drained medium. Keep it evenly

SAXIFRAGA STOLONIFERA

SCHLUMBERGERA BRIDGESII

SCILLA SIBERICA

SENECIO × HYBRIDUS

moist except in fall after lowering the temperature to set flower buds; then the medium should be allowed to dry slightly between waterings. As soon as flower buds form, resume normal watering and return the plant to a warm room. Flower buds will drop if the medium is too dry or too wet, or if light or humidity is too low. Fertilize monthly in spring and summer, and when plants are flowering. To ensure that a Christmas cactus blooms for Christmas, place the plants in a cool room in mid-September and place them in complete darkness for 16 hours per night until mid-October; then return them to normal conditions. To ensure that a Thanksgiving cactus blooms for Thanksgiving, place it in a cool room in mid-August and provide complete darkness for 12 hours each night until mid-September, before returning it to normal growing conditions. To force either plant to bloom at other times of year, manipulate the light similarly, starting approximately three months ahead of the date on which you want the plant to bloom. Both Thanksgiving and Christmas cacti can be propagated from stem cuttings in spring or from seed. They can be attacked by spider mites and are susceptible to rot and wilt diseases.

Scilla (SIL-a)
Squill

Spring-flowering bulb that can be forced into bloom in winter and early spring for use indoors. The leaves grow from the base of the plant. The flowers are white, purple or blue, and bloom in spikes.

Selected species and varieties. *S. siberica,* Siberian squill, grows 6 inches high and has two to five strap-shaped leaves. The flowers are bell-shaped, ½ inch across, waxy, drooping and deep blue, and bloom in spikes. 'Alba' has white flowers. 'Azurea' has bright blue flowers. 'Taurica' has light blue flowers with dark midveins.

Growing conditions. Siberian squill can be purchased in bloom, or you can force your own bulbs after subjecting them to a chilling period. To do this, plant bulbs in fall in a well-drained, soilless medium. Water well and place the pots outside, either buried in the ground or protected in a cold frame, for 10 weeks. If the temperature does not drop below 40° F during this period, place the bulbs in a refrigerator to chill. Put the pots in a room where temperature is cool, light is bright to direct and humidity is high. Keep the growing medium evenly moist, and do not fertilize. After the plants have flowered, discard the bulbs. The small bulblets that form around the main bulb can be removed and potted to start new plants. Aphids may attack; bulbs may be susceptible to rot diseases.

Sea onion see *Ornithogalum*

Senecio (se-NEE-see-o)

One of the largest genera of flowering plants, containing annuals and perennials, some of which are grown as houseplants. All produce daisy- or button-like flowers.

Selected species and varieties. *S. × hybridus,* cineraria, grows to 12 inches high and forms a crown of 3- to 4-inch, heart-shaped to oval, hairy leaves. Flowers are velvety; daisylike; 1 to 4 inches across; white, pink, red, blue or purple, sometimes with a circle of white on the center of the petals; and bloom in immense clusters. Plants are grown to flower in winter and spring.

Growing conditions. Place cineraria in a cool room where light is bright and humidity is high. Grow in well-drained, soilless medium and keep it evenly moist. Fertilizing is not necessary. After the plant has flowered, it will deteriorate and should be discarded. New plants are grown from seed. Plants can be attacked by aphids, mealybugs, spider mites, whiteflies, virus, mildew, botrytis blight, and root and stem rot.

—

Shrimp plant see *Justicia*

Shrub verbena see *Lantana*

Siberian squill see *Scilla*

—

SINNINGIA SPECIOSA

Sinningia (si-NIN-jee-a)

Genus of tuberous flowering plants in the gesneriad family. Leaves are basal; flowers are bell-shaped to cylindrical and open into five lobes.

Selected species and varieties. *S. regina,* slipper gloxinia, has oval, velvety, dark green leaves that are veined with white on the top surfaces and deep red on the undersides. The flowers are nodding and violet, have a curved tube and bloom on thin, leafless stems. *S. speciosa,* gloxinia, grows up to 12 inches high and has oval to oblong, 8-inch, broad, hairy leaves. The flowers are lavender, rose, pink, red, white or yellow; are often banded or spotted; and bloom mostly in summer. New varieties may bloom at any time of year. The flowers appear in clusters in the center of the plant, and are trumpet-shaped with frilled edges. Some varieties have double flowers.

Growing conditions. Gloxinias like warm temperature, bright light and high humidity. Plant the tubers in a rich, soilless medium, and keep it evenly moist while the plants are growing or flowering. Fertilize every month during the growing and flowering period. After the flowers fade, withhold water and allow the foliage to die down. Store the tubers in a dry medium; repot them when new growth appears, in two to four months, and start the process over again. New plants can be grown from division, by leaf cuttings or from seed. Gloxinias can be attacked by aphids, spider mites, thrips, virus, and root, leaf and crown rot.

—

Solanum (so-LAY-num)

Genus of annuals and perennials that includes potato and eggplant. Although the genus contains edible plants, some species are toxic. Plants have round to bell-shaped, five-lobed flowers that are often followed by colorful fruit.

SOLANUM PSEUDOCAPSICUM

SPATHIPHYLLUM × HYBRIDUM

Selected species and varieties. *S. pseudocapsicum,* Jerusalem cherry, is a shrubby plant that grows about 12 inches high indoors. The leaves are oblong to lance-shaped, 2 inches long and glossy green, often with wavy margins. The flowers are white, star-shaped, small and not showy, and appear in summer; the plant is grown for its round, red or yellow, ½-inch fruits. Plants are usually grown so they are in fruit for the winter holidays. 'Patersonii' has a spreading habit and fruits abundantly.

Growing conditions. Place Jerusalem cherry in a room where temperature is average to warm, light is direct and humidity is average. The fruit will shrivel and dry out quickly if the room is too warm. The growing medium should be well drained and allowed to dry slightly between waterings. Fertilize every two weeks. After the fruit has fallen, cut the plant back by one-half; it will benefit from being placed outdoors for the summer. Shake plants when they are flowering to aid in pollination and fruit set. Plants will not form satisfactory fruit for more than two years, and should be discarded after the second season. The fruit of Jerusalem cherry is poisonous. New plants are grown from seed sown in early spring for fruit the following winter. Jerusalem cherries are subject to attack by aphids, scales, whiteflies, leaf spot, virus and wilt.

—

Spanish-shawl see *Heterocentron*
Spathe flower see *Spathiphyllum*

—

Spathiphyllum (spath-i-FIL-um)
Spathe flower, white flag, peace lily

Tropical perennial that can be grown indoors. The leaves are glossy green and oblong. The flowers are white, fragrant and tiny, and bloom along a tail-like structure called a spadix. The spadix is surrounded by a white or green bract called a spathe. Flowers appear most abundantly in spring and summer.

Selected species and varieties. *S. clevelandii,* white anthurium, has narrow, 12-inch leaves, an oval, 6-inch white spathe and a 2-inch spadix. Plants may reach 3 feet in height. *S. × hybridum* is a group of hybrids that have narrow, oblong, 10-inch leaves and grow to 2½ feet high. The spathes are large and white and have green midribs on the undersides. 'Mauna Loa' is a compact, very floriferous hybrid growing 2 to 3 feet high and having 8- to 10-inch very dark green leaves and 4- to 5-inch spathes.

Growing conditions. Grow spathe flower where temperature is warm, light is limited to bright and humidity is medium to high. Plant in soilless growing medium and keep it evenly moist at all times. Fertilize every two weeks from spring through fall. Dust or wash the foliage frequently. Plants can be divided at any time of year. Spathe flower is not troubled by insects but is susceptible to leaf spot diseases.

—

Spider lily see *Crinum; Lycoris*
Spurge see *Euphorbia*

Squill see *Scilla*

Star cluster see *Pentas*

Star jasmine see *Trachelospermum*

Star-of-Bethlehem
see *Campanula; Ornithogalum*

—

Stephanotis (stef-a-NO-tis)

Genus of vining plants, one species of which is grown as a houseplant. The leaves are leathery; the flowers are fragrant and funnel-shaped, open into five lobes and bloom in clusters.

Selected species and varieties. *S. floribunda,* Madagascar jasmine, wax flower, can grow up to 15 feet tall, but usually grows much smaller in the house. The leaves are elliptic, pointed, thick, shiny and 2 to 4 inches long. The flowers are white, waxy, fragrant and 1 to 2 inches long. They bloom in 4- to 6-inch clusters in spring and summer.

Growing conditions. Grow Madagascar jasmine in a warm room with direct light and moderate humidity. Plants should be grown in well-drained, soilless medium; keep the medium evenly moist from midspring to midfall. From midfall to midspring, allow the medium to dry slightly between waterings. Fertilize monthly from midspring to midfall. Plants need to be trained on a trellis, a wire hoop or other support. Pinch back growing tips to keep plants bushy. Propagate from stem cuttings or from seed. Scales and mealybugs are the primary insects that attack Madagascar jasmine; botrytis blight is the primary disease.

—

Strawberry geranium see *Saxifraga*

—

Strelitzia (stre-LITS-ee-a)
Bird-of-paradise

Subtropical perennial that can be grown as a houseplant. The leaves are large and erect, and grow in clumps from the base of the plant. The flowers grow from a rigid, green, boatlike bract and resemble the head of an exotic bird.

Selected species and varieties. *S. reginae* grows 3 to 6 feet tall. Leaves are 1 to 1½ feet long, stiff, oblong, leathery, pointed, and blue-green with a yellow or red midrib. The flowers have orange or yellow petals and a deep blue tongue that emerges from the bract, which is edged in purple or red.

Growing conditions. Place bird-of-paradise in a room where temperature is average, light is direct and humidity is medium to high. Plants should be grown in soilless, well-drained medium that is allowed to dry out slightly between waterings in winter and is kept barely moist the rest of the year. Fertilize every two weeks during spring and summer. Plants may be propagated by division, from suckers or from seed, but those grown from seed take sev-

STEPHANOTIS FLORIBUNDA

STRELITZIA REGINAE

STREPTOCARPUS × HYBRIDUS

THUNBERGIA ALATA

eral years before they bloom. Bird-of-paradise is susceptible to scales, mealybugs and root rot.

—

Streptocarpus (strep-toh-KAR-pus)
Cape primrose

Large genus of annuals and perennials in the gesneriad family. Flowers are funnel-shaped, five-lobed and bloom throughout the year, but most abundantly in late spring through fall.

Selected species and varieties. *S. × hybridus* is a large group of hybrids that have 10- to 12-inch, oblong, scalloped, wrinkled leaves that grow in a rosette at the base of the plant. The flowers are 2 to 5 inches long and nodding, and may be white, pink, rose, red, blue or purple, often with a throat of a contrasting color. The flowers bloom in small clusters at the top of thin, leafless stems. *S. saxorum,* dauphin violet, has oval, 1¼-inch leaves and lavender, tubular flowers.

Growing conditons. *S. × hybridus* likes a spot where temperature is cool in winter and average the rest of the year. The light should be bright, the humidity high. Grow in well-drained, rich, soilless medium, and from spring through fall, keep it evenly moist. In winter, water only enough to keep the plant from wilting. Fertilize twice a month during spring and summer. *S. saxorum* does not go dormant the way *S. × hybridus* does, and so should remain in a room with average temperature and in an evenly moist medium all year. Plants can be fertilized all year as well. For both species, use a shallow pot to help reduce the chance of root rot. Grow new plants of *S. × hybridus* by division in winter, from leaf cuttings taken in spring or summer, or from seed sown in winter or spring. *S. saxorum* is propagated from stem cuttings or from seed. Aphids, mealybugs and thrips may attack; root rot is the most common disease.

—

Tailflower see *Anthurium*
Thanksgiving cactus see *Schlumbergera*

—

Thunbergia (thun-BER-jee-a)

Genus of erect and vining perennials and shrubs, one species of which is often grown as a houseplant. The flowers are large and showy and have five lobes.

Selected species and varieties. *T. alata,* black-eyed Susan vine, is a twining, 2- to 6-foot plant that has triangular to oval, 1- to 3-inch, toothed leaves. The flowers are 1 to 2 inches across and single, and white, creamy white, pale yellow or orange, usually dark at the center. Plants bloom in spring and summer. 'Alba' has white flowers with dark centers. 'Aurantica' has orange-yellow flowers with dark centers. 'Bakeri' has pure white flowers.

Growing conditions. Grow black-eyed Susan vine in a room where temperature is average to warm, light is direct and humidity is average. The growing medium should be soilless and well drained, and constantly moist when the plant is flowering. At other times, let the medium dry out slightly between waterings. Fertilize every two weeks during spring and summer. For the vines, provide a trellis or other support, or let the plants cascade out of hanging baskets. After a plant has flowered, cut it back to several inches. If it starts to deteriorate, it should be discarded. New plants may be propagated from seed, from stem cuttings or by layering. Mealybugs and scales are the major attacking insects. Black-eyed Susan vine is generally free of diseases.

Tibouchina (tib-o-KY-na)
Glory bush

Tropical shrub, one species of which is grown as a houseplant. The leaves have three to seven prominent veins; the flowers are large and showy.

Selected species and varieties. *T. urvilleana* grows 4 to 6 feet high indoors. The leaves are oval to oblong, 2 to 4 inches long, finely toothed, bristly on the upper surfaces and hairy on the undersides. The flowers are single, five-petaled, 2 inches across, rose-purple to violet, and have purple stamens.

Growing conditions. Grow glory bush in a room with average temperature, bright light and medium humidity. The growing medium should be well drained, soilless and evenly moist at all times. Fertilize every month during spring and summer. New plants can be grown from stem cuttings. Scales are the most common insect pests; root rot is the primary disease.

Tiger orchid see *Odontoglossum*

Tillandsia (ti-LAND-zee-a

Large genus in the bromeliad family, many species of which are suitable for houseplants. The leaves are grasslike, grow in a dense rosette at the base of the plant and form a cup that can hold water. One showy flower at a time emerges from a flat spike of bracts.

Selected species and varieties. *T. caput-Medusae,* Medusa's head, grows 10 inches tall from a bulbous stem base. Leaves are long, fleshy, straplike and gray to gray-green. The bracts are red, pink or green; the flowers are purple. *T. cyanea* grows 10 inches high and has 14-inch narrow, recurved leaves that have red-brown lines. The bracts are pink, rose or red; the flowers are deep violet, 1 inch across, have spreading petals and bloom in short, broad, flat spikes. *T. lindenii* grows 2½ feet high and has arching, 16-inch, narrow leaves. The flower spike is erect and narrow and has green or rose-colored bracts. The flowers are deep blue and 2 inches long or longer.

Growing conditions. These tillandsias prefer warm temperatures, bright light and high humidity. The growing medium should be soilless, well drained and extra coarse; keep it barely moist at all times. Make sure that there is always water in the cup at the base of the plant. Fertilize monthly with quarter-strength liquid fertilizer. Start new plants by removing and planting the offshoots that grow at the base of the plant after it has flowered. Tillandsia is susceptible to scales and to crown rot.

TIBOUCHINA URVILLEANA

TILLANDSIA CAPUT-MEDUSAE

133

TRACHELOSPERMUM JASMINOIDES

TROPAEOLUM MAJUS

Trachelospermum (tra-ke-lo-SPER-mum)

Genus of tropical and subtropical vines that can be grown indoors. The flowers are white, tubular, fragrant, star-shaped, ½ to 1 inch across, and bloom in loose clusters in spring and summer. The leaves are oblong, leathery and 1½ to 2½ inches long. Plants may grow to 8 feet indoors but can be kept smaller.

Selected species and varieties. *T. asiaticum,* Japanese star jasmine, has yellowish white flowers with dark throats. *T. jasminoides,* star jasmine, Confederate star jasmine, has white flowers with wavy lobes. 'Japonicum' has white-veined leaves. 'Variegatum' has leaves variegated in green and white, and often tinted in red.

Growing conditions. Grow trachelospermum in a room with cool to average temperature, bright light and medium to high humidity. The growing medium should be soilless and well drained, and allowed to dry slightly between waterings. Fertilize every two to three months. Trachelospermum can be grown on a trellis or other support, but frequent pinching of the growing tips will result in a bushy plant that does not need support. Plants benefit from being moved outdoors in summer. Propagate from stem cuttings taken in fall. Scales and whiteflies sometimes attack; so do the diseases leaf spot and root rot.

—

Transvaal daisy see *Gerbera*
Treasure flower see *Gazania*

—

Tropaeolum (tro-PEE-o-lum)
Nasturtium

Genus of bushy and vining perennials and annuals, one species of which can be grown as a houseplant. The leaves are lobed; the flowers are yellow, red or orange.

Selected species and varieties. *T. majus* is an annual having round, dull green leaves that are 2 to 7 inches across and appear on long stalks. The flowers are 2½ to 3½ inches across, fragrant, single or double, and often spotted or striped. Plants may be either vining or bushy, depending on the variety, and grow to 2 feet high and wide indoors. 'Nana Compacta' is a dwarf variety that grows to 12 inches high and wide. The plant is edible and has a peppery flavor. Flower buds and seeds are used as seasonings and garnishes; the leaves can be used in salads.

Growing conditions. Grow nasturtium where temperature is cool, light is direct and humidity is moderate. The medium should be soilless, sandy, well drained and evenly moist at all times. After the flower buds have formed, fertilize monthly; fertilizing prematurely results in lush foliage and few flowers. Vining varieties may be grown in hanging baskets. Pinch plants occasionally to keep them compact. After a plant has flowered, it will die and should be discarded. Nasturtiums may be propagated from seed or from stem cuttings and will flower in three to six months. Aphids, thrips, spider mites and leaf spot may attack.

Tulip see *Tulipa*

—

Tulipa (TOO-lip-a)
Tulip

Spring-flowering bulb that can be forced to bloom indoors in winter. The leaves are dull green, lance-shaped and pointed, and grow from the base of the plant and along the flower stems. The flowers may be single or double and are available in all colors.

Selected species and varieties. There are hundreds of hybrid tulip varieties. Those most often forced into bloom for use as houseplants are the cottage tulips, which have single, egg-shaped flowers and grow 1½ to 2½ feet tall; Darwin tulips, which have single flowers with square bases and grow 2 to 2½ feet tall; single early tulips, which have single, egg-shaped flowers and grow 10 to 16 inches tall; parrot tulips, which have large, fringed flowers that bloom on 2-foot stems; and double early and double late tulips, which have double flowers and grow 8 to 16 inches tall. They look the same, but the double earlies bloom sooner than the double lates.

Growing conditions. Tulips may be purchased in bloom, or you can force your own bulbs. To force your own, pot the bulbs in fall in a well-drained, soilless medium, and place five to six bulbs in a 6-inch pot. Plant the bulbs with the flat side against the rim of the pot. The tip of the bulb should be just below the medium. Place the pot outdoors, either protected in a cold frame or buried in the ground. If temperatures do not drop below 40° F, the pot must be refrigerated. Let it remain chilled for 12 to 16 weeks, or until the bulbs have 2 to 3 inches of top growth. Move the pot to a room where the temperature is cool, light is direct and humidity is medium to high. Keep the medium evenly moist. Fertilizing is not necessary. Tall varieties may be staked. After the tulips have finished blooming, discard them. It is difficult to propagate your own bulbs, so start with newly purchased bulbs every year. Among the insects and diseases to which tulips are susceptible are spider mites, aphids, fusarium, botrytis blight and virus.

—

Urn plant see *Aechmea*
Vase plant see *Billbergia*

—

Vriesea (VREE-zhee-a)

Genus of bromeliads with stiff, strap-shaped leaves that grow in basal rosettes. In the center of the plant is a cup that holds water. The leaves are often banded or variegated in red or brown. The flowers bloom in flat spikes and have conspicuous bracts.

Selected species and varieties. *V. guttata,* painted feather, grows 16 inches high and has narrow, 10-inch blue-green leaves that are spotted in maroon or brown. The flowers are yellow and the bracts are greenish beige suffused with bright silvery pink. The flower spikes are pendulous and bloom from late winter to early summer. *V. splendens,* flaming sword, grows to 3 feet in height and

TULIPA HYBRID

VRIESEA SPLENDENS

ZANTEDESCHIA ELLIOTTIANA

has 16-inch blue-green leaves with brown or purple crossbands. The flowers are yellow; the bracts are bright red. The flower spikes are erect and bloom in spring and summer.

Growing conditions. Grow vriesea where temperature is average or warm, light is bright and humidity is medium. The potting medium should be soilless, coarse and allowed to dry slightly between waterings. Be sure there is always water in the cup at the base of the plant. Fertilize monthly by adding fertilizer solution to the water in the cup. Propagate by removing the side shoots that develop at the base of the plant. Scales and crown rot may attack.

Water willow see *Justicia*

Wax begonia see *Begonia*

Wax flower see *Stephanotis*

Wax plant see *Hoya*

Wax vine see *Hoya*

White anthurium see *Spathiphyllum*

White flag see *Spathiphyllum*

Widow's tears see *Achimenes*

Wonder flower see *Ornithogalum*

Yellow sage see *Lantana*

Yesterday-today-and-tomorrow
see *Brunfelsia*

Zantedeschia (zan-te-DES-kee-a)
Calla lily

Rhizomatous plant that has arrow-shaped leaves. Flowers consist of a spadix surrounded by a showy, colorful spathe. The spathe flares back at the top, and the edges curl under. The flowers appear from fall through spring.

Selected species and varieties. *Z. aethiopica,* florist's calla, grows to 3 feet tall and has 18-inch leaves. The spathe is white and 5 to 10 inches long. The spadix has fragrant yellow flowers. 'Childsiana' is similar in appearance but grows 1½ feet tall. *Z. albomaculata,* spotted calla, grows 3 feet high and has 18-inch leaves that are spotted in white. The spathe is 4½ inches long and white to pale yellow. The base of the spathe is marked in purple. *Z. elliottiana,* golden calla, grows 2 feet high and has 2-foot leaves that are spotted in white. The spathe is 6 inches long, bright yellow on the inside and greenish yellow on the outside. *Z. rehmannii,* pink calla, grows 2 feet high and has narrow 12-inch leaves that are sometimes spotted in white. The spathe is 5 inches long and pink, rose or purple.

Growing conditions. Grow calla lilies where light is bright and humidity is average. Florist's calla likes a cool temperature; the others prefer average temperature. The medium should be soilless, rich, well drained and constantly moist. Fertilize monthly after the flowers appear. After the plant has finished flowering, allow the medium to dry out between waterings for several months to give the plant a rest. Plants may be allowed to go completely dormant in summer; if they are to remain growing, place them in bright light. Propagate new plants by division in late summer or early fall, by removing the offshoots or from seed. Mealybugs, spider mites and root rot may attack.

—

Zebra plant see *Aphelandra*

—

Zephyranthes (zef-i-RAN-theez)
Zephyr lily, rain lily

Summer-flowering bulb that may be grown as a houseplant to bloom at any time of year. The leaves are grassy and grow from the base of the plant in an arching habit. The flowers are funnel-shaped, six-petaled, upward-facing and bloom one to a stem.

Selected species and varieties. *Z. atamasco,* Atamasco lily, grows 12 inches high. The leaves are narrow and have sharp edges. The flowers are 3 inches across and white, sometimes tinged with purple. *Z. candida* has slightly fleshy 1-foot leaves and 2-inch flowers that are white, occasionally pinkish, shaded green near the base. *Z. grandiflora* grows 12 inches high and has flat leaves. The flowers are 4 inches wide and rose or pink.

Growing conditions. Give zephyr lily a spot where temperature is cool, light is direct and humidity is medium to high. Grow in a soilless medium and keep it evenly moist while the plant is growing and flowering. Fertilize monthly. After the flowers have faded and the foliage has started to turn brown, withhold water for two or three months to let the plant rest, then resume watering and fertilizing. Plants will bloom in about 10 weeks. Propagate by removing and potting the small bulblets that form around the base of the main bulb. Scales may attack; leaf spot and rot may develop.

—

Zephyr lily see *Zephyranthes*

ZEPHYRANTHES CANDIDA

PICTURE CREDITS

FURTHER READING

Bailey, Liberty Hyde, and Ethel Zoe Bailey, *Hortus Third: A Concise Dictionary of Plants Cultivated in the United States and Canada.* New York: Macmillan, 1976.

Beckett, Kenneth A., *The Royal Horticultural Society Encyclopedia of House Plants.* Boston: Salem House, 1987.

Brookes, John, *The Indoor Garden Book.* New York: Crown Publishers, 1986.

Crockett, James Underwood, *Crockett's Indoor Garden.* Boston: Little, Brown and Company, 1978.

Davidson, William, and T. C. Rochford, *The Complete All-Color Guide to House Plants Cacti and Succulents.* New York, Galahad Books, 1976.

Ferguson, Barbara J., ed., *All about Houseplants.* San Francisco: Ortho Books/Chevron Chemical Company, 1982.

Herwig, Rob, *How to Grow Healthy House Plants.* Los Angeles: HP Books, 1979.

James, Theodore, Jr., *African Violets and Other Gesneriads: How to Select and Grow.* Los Angeles: HP Books, 1983.

Kramer, Jack, *Growing Hybrid Orchids Indoors.* New York: Universe Books, 1983.

March, Ken, *Houseplants for Free.* Secaucus, New Jersey: Chartwell Books, 1988.

Northen, Rebecca Tyson, *Home Orchid Growing.* New York: Van Nostrand Reinhold, 1970.

Reader's Digest Editors, *Success with House Plants.* Pleasantville, New York: Reader's Digest Association, 1979.

Scott, George Harmon, *Bulbs: How to Select, Grow and Enjoy.* Los Angeles: HP Books, 1982.

Seddon, George, *Your Indoor Garden.* New York: Exeter Books, 1984.

Seddon, George, and Andrew Bicknell, *The Essential Guide to Perfect Houseplants.* New York: Summit Books, 1984.

Sessler, Gloria Jean, *Orchids and How to Grow Them.* New York: Prentice Hall Press, 1978.

Shakery, Karin, *Ortho's Complete Guide to Successful Houseplants.* San Francisco: Ortho Books/Chevron Chemical Company, 1984.

Simpson, A.G.W., *The Colorful World of African Violets.* London: Tiger Books International, 1978.

Smith, Michael D., ed., *All about Bulbs.* San Francisco: Ortho Books/Chevron Chemical Company, 1986.

Taylor, Norman, *Taylor's Guide to Houseplants.* Boston: Houghton Mifflin, 1987.

Wright, Michael, *The Complete Indoor Gardener.* New York: Random House, 1979.

ACKNOWLEDGMENTS

The index for this book was prepared by Lee McKee.
The editors also wish to thank: Jane Birge, African Violet Society of America, Beaumont, Texas; Mary Boland, African Violet Society of America, Alexandria, Virginia; Maria Brown, Bethesda, Maryland; The Corner Garden, Middleburg, Virginia; Dr. Morgan Delaney, Alexandria, Virginia; Galen Goss, National Chrysanthemum Society, Fairfax Station, Virginia; Richard D. Grundy, Alexandria, Virginia; Kenneth E. Hancock, Annandale, Virginia; Julie Harris, Arlington, Virginia; Hillbrook Inn, Charles Town, West Virginia; Merrit Huntington, Kensington Orchids, Kensington, Maryland; Lyndon Lyon, Greenhouses, Inc., Dolgeville, New York; Thanh Huu Nguyen, Alexandria, Virginia; Phil Normandy and Bob Rinker, Brookside Gardens, Wheaton, Maryland; Patrick Nutt, Longwood Gardens, Kennett Square, Pennsylvania; Bev Promersberger, Annandale, Virginia; Jayne E. Rohrich, Alexandria, Virginia; Jos and Eric Roozen, Roozen Nursery, Fort Washington, Maryland; Dr. Laurence E. Skog, National Museum of Natural History, Smithsonian Institution, Washington, D.C.; U.S. Botanic Garden, Washington, D.C.

INDEX

*Numerals in italics indicate an illustration
of the subject mentioned.*

REDEFINITION

Senior Editors	Anne Horan, Robert G. Mason
Design Director	Robert Barkin
Designer	Edwina Smith
Illustration	Nicholas Fasciano
Assistant Designers	Sue Pratt, Monique Strawderman
Picture Editor	Deborah Thornton
Production Editor	Anthony K. Pordes
Editorial Research	Gail Prensky, (volume coordinator), Barbara B. Smith, Mary Yee, Elizabeth D. McLean
Picture Research	Caroline N. Tell
Text Editor	Carol Gardner
Writers	Gerald Jonas, Ann Reilly David S. Thomson
Administration	Margaret M. Higgins, June M. Nolan
Finance Director	Vaughn A. Meglan
PRESIDENT	Edward Brash

Time-Life Books Inc.
is a wholly owned subsidiary of

THE TIME INC. BOOK COMPANY

President and Chief Executive Officer	Kelso F. Sutton
President, Time Inc. Books Direct	Christopher T. Linen

TIME-LIFE BOOKS INC.

EDITOR	George Constable
Executive Editor	Ellen Phillips
Director of Design	Louis Klein
Director of Editorial Resources	Phyllis K. Wise
Director of Photography and Research	John Conrad Weiser
PRESIDENT	John M. Fahey Jr.
Senior Vice Presidents	Robert M. DeSena, Paul R. Stewart, Curtis G. Viebranz, Joseph J. Ward
Vice Presidents	Stephen L. Bair, Bonita L. Boezeman, Mary P. Donohoe, Stephen L. Goldstein, Juanita T. James, Andrew P. Kaplan, Trevor Lunn, Susan J. Maruyama, Robert H. Smith
New Product Development	Yuri Okuda, Donia Ann Steele
Supervisor of Quality Control	James King
PUBLISHER	Joseph J. Ward

Editorial Operations

Copy Chief	Diane Ullius
Production	Celia Beattie
Library	Louise D. Forstall
Computer Composition	Gordon E. Buck (Manager), Deborah G. Tait, Monika D. Thayer, Janet Barnes Syring, Lillian Daniels
Correspondents	Elisabeth Kraemer-Singh (Bonn), Christina Lieberman (New York), Maria Vincenza Aloisi (Paris), Ann Natanson (Rome)

THE CONSULTANTS

C. Colston Burrell is the series consultant for The Time-Life Gardener's Guide and special consultant for *Wildflowers*. He is Curator of Plant Collections at the Minnesota Landscape Arboretum, part of the University of Minnesota. He was formerly Curator of Native Plant Collections at the National Arboretum in Washington, D.C., and is the author of publications about ferns and wildflowers.

A. J. Lewis is the consultant for *Flowering Houseplants*. He is Director of the State Botanical Garden of Georgia, has taught horticulture at the University of Georgia, Virginia Polytechnic Institute and State University, and Clemson University, and has published numerous articles on flowering plants.

Library of Congress Cataloging-in-Publication Data
Flowering house plants
    p. cm.—(The Time-Life gardener's guide)
    Bibliograpy: p.
    Includes index.
    ISBN 0-8094-6652-X.—ISBN 0-8094-6653-8 (lib. bdg.)
    1. House plants. 2. Flowers. 3.Indoor gardening
I. Time-Life Books. II. Series.
SB419.F555 1990 635.9'65—dc20 89-20315 CIP

Time-Life Books Inc. offers a wide range of fine recordings, including a *Rock 'n' Roll Era* series. For subscription information, call 1-800-621-7026, or write Time-Life Music, P.O. Box C-32068, Richmond, Virginia 23261-2068.